Best Wishes,

Jack W. Plunkett

NEW AMERICAN LIGHT CUISINE

**Other Books
by Jude W. Theriot**

*La Cuisine Cajun (1986)
La Meilleure de la Louisiane (1986)*

New American Light Cuisine

Jude W. Theriot

Pelican Publishing Company
GRETNA **1988**

Library of Congress Cataloging-in-Publication Data
Theriot, Jude W.
  New American light cuisine.

  Includes index.
  1. Low-calorie diet—Recipes. I. Title.
RM 222.2.T475   1988   641.5'635   87-32841
ISBN 0-88289-690-3

Manufactured in the United States of America

Published by Pelican Publishing Company, Inc.
1101 Monroe Street, Gretna, Louisiana 70053

To Joyce Bilbray, Assistant to the Publisher, Pelican Publishing Company, for bringing me into the Pelican family. I will always appreciate your kindness and sincere interest in my work. Thanks a million!

To Kathleen Calhoun, Promotion Director, Pelican Publishing Company, for your constant "urging" me to finish this book! I do appreciate your support and strong encouragement to get this job done. Thanks for helping me see it through.

To James Calhoun, Executive Editor, Pelican Publishing Company, and Vilma Calhoun, for your care in editing and your suggestions and insights into what makes a book "work." Thanks for taking the time to aim me in the right direction.

To Milburn Calhoun, Publisher and President, Pelican Publishing Company, and Nancy Calhoun, Vice-President, Pelican Publishing Company, for your faith in me and your guidance through the tasks of writing cookbooks. I sincerely appreciate all you have done for me and my books. No publisher could equal your genuineness or caring. Thanks for your support and your confidence.

And a special dedication to the memory of Polly Theriot Baudean, my previous editor, whose work on La Cuisine Cajun *and whose sweet and pleasant personality will remain with me always.*

Contents

Introduction

Why on earth would anyone write a low-calorie cookbook? You might be asking yourself that question right now. I know I did! For years, low-calorie meant low quality or no taste to me. Quite by accident, however, I discovered that dishes with great taste can also be low in caloric content. When I was writing my second book, *La Cuisine Cajun*, the promotion director for Pelican Publishing Company, Kathleen Calhoun, really insisted on a calorie count for the book. I thought she was crazy, a calorie count for Cajun food! What I found out from doing the calorie count has changed my thinking and changed my eating habits for good.

I found out that many of my old ideas about "dieting" were for the birds! Always in the past when I decided to diet, I would give up all the things I liked. I quit eating such dishes as rice, potatoes, and pasta and ate more meat. I really believed high protein was the way to go. Those diets worked well, but only for a short time, then back came the weight. Dieting has a negative meaning for me! It means giving up, so it is doomed to failure before you start. This is NOT A DIET BOOK! If you think you are buying a diet book and that is what you want, put this book back. It is a book of recipes that gives you calorie counts and other dietary information that can be useful by helping you to change your eating patterns. Dieting just doesn't work. If you are like me, you may have tried all the diet fads that came around. You probably found out that 99 percent of them worked. Then after being on one of the "fad diets" for a while you'd go "crazy" and eat everything in sight, but mainly the foods that are off your diet plan. Or you lose the weight you set out to lose, resume your old eating habits, and promptly gain it all back.

I will never diet again! This book is about NOT DIETING. I forever give up any type of diet, fad or not. (At least until they invent the "fat removal room"—you know what room I'm talking about. You walk in fat, sit down, and someone turns a switch and one minute later you walk out slim and fit—it's every fat person's dream.) I write down everything that goes into my mouth, calculate the calories, and stop eating when my calorie count reaches the level I have predetermined for the day. I try to keep my calorie count at 1,500 calories per day for four days a week and at 2,000 calories per day for the other three days a week. This seems to work for me. The number of calories you can have per day to lose weight or maintain your weight will vary. I suggest you see your physician to help you set up your calorie plan and to make sure you can lose weight safely.

Do eat a balanced diet. Eat breakfast every day. Drink plenty of water, about eight eight-ounce glasses per day. Plan some type of moderate exercise program with your doctor's supervision; it might be walking, swimming, or biking, but be sure it is something. Exercise helps to boost the metabolism to burn more calories; you have to do it if you are going to succeed. Be sure to keep an accurate count of your caloric intake. You cannot guess. Write everything down to be sure you are following your plan. That will help you to answer wisely questions such as:

"Do I really want that glass of orange juice for 110 calories?"

"Is a glass of wine really worth 80 calories?"

"I think I'll have that piece of chocolate cake with chocolate icing for 233 calories, since I've got the calories left to spend and it is really what I want today."

Such choices don't mean giving up what you like. You can choose the type of food you like most, but in moderation and with good sense. It does mean you have to have will power. You will have to be able to stop when you reach the total calorie cap for the day. I have found that just writing my calories down as I eat them is a great help. Try eating just as you always do, but writing down everything you put into your mouth. You will soon see you are not just gaining weight for no reason. Don't ever believe you can just look at food and gain weight; it doesn't happen that way. I carry around a small memo book to jot down everything in. You will be amazed how writing down foods also helps you become conscious of your eating habits. It forces you to make a decision and prevents eating food by habit or reflex. Remember, be honest with yourself; it is the only way you will succeed. You can hide your eating habits from everyone but yourself.

Rather than dieting, restructure your lifestyle. Take charge of your eating habits by counting your calories and any other specific dietary information you may need to count (*e.g.*, fat, cholesterol). This is an ever changing process. Don't try it for a few weeks, do it for life . . . your life! Eat a balanced diet, but be sure to include your likes, all of them. Just don't overdo any one item or go over your total calorie count for the day.

How will you know if you are in need of restructuring your eating habits? You'll know it's time to begin some type of structured eating program if you hear anyone say one of the following things about you, either behind your back or to your face:

1. You carry your weight so well!
2. Yes, but you are big boned, you can take all that extra weight!
3. Do you have a scale at home?

Here is another sure sign the time has come to begin a new plan. Look around your house. If you can't find a mirror anywhere, the time is now. DO IT FOR YOU! All too often, overweight people are encouraged by others to lose weight. That works only for a short while. When you are ready to do it for yourself, you will succeed.

If you fail or fall, don't give up. Get up and get back on track. You can "cheat" on a diet, but you can't cheat yourself. Don't get bogged down asking, "Why am I fat?" We really don't know everything about weight loss and gain yet. In fact, we are just scratching the surface, but all that research into why, won't get you results. For now, just count your calories and you'll get good results. To lose weight you have to be able to eat regular food that can be cooked and eaten everyday. It can be exciting food. Be creative! Remember, variety is one of the best spices you can add to your diet. Look for the different. Change things so you don't get bored or get those "cravings" that destroy diets.

I wish I could tell you I've changed for good and now it is easy to keep to a schedule. I have not and it is still not easy. I'm still waiting for the day (just like you are) that my metabolism will change and I'll be able to eat everything I want as often and as much as I want. I know that is not likely to happen, so I will have to structure my eating habits so I can eat what I want as long as I eat within my daily caloric allowance. That may mean one or two cookies instead of ten or more, but at least I can have them. I try not to look at what I can't have, but rather I look at all I can now have.

You just have to count everything. Don't even think of cheating! If the recipe calls for a small potato, don't use a large one and think you really put one over. A small potato is counted as 90 calories; use a small potato. Don't be tempted to add calories by playing a game with sizes called for in the recipes. You'll only hurt yourself. If you go into a restaurant that has a happy hour, remember a price break or "two for one" doesn't apply to calories.

Use this cookbook as a starting point for changing your eating habits. It will help you to organize your meals and give you information you can use to plan your meals. Plan in advance what you are going to cook and serve. Please feel free to substitute. I offer you many suggestions in the lagniappe section of each recipe. Try some of my suggestions and then create some new ones yourself. Even when you count calories, cooking and eating should and can be enjoyable. There are so many new products available on the market that help to add flavor and variety to our menus. Look for them, have a great time cooking, and then enjoy your meals. Good cooking should be a part of any weight loss program, because it will help you stick to your plan. I hope these recipes that follow will encourage you and delight you. Bon appetit and good luck!

Why Count Calories?

Why count calories? The answer is very simple: calories count! Calories are the chief enemy when it comes to losing weight. You put on only what you put into your mouth as calories. There is much new research going on about dieting and weight loss, but the bottom line is calories. If you eat more than your body needs to maintain itself, you are going to gain weight.

The key is finding out what your body needs to maintain your weight and giving it constantly less than that amount. Consult your physician to calculate the calories you need per day to maintain your weight, and the calories per day you can eat and lose weight. Once you have that important information, you are ready to begin a lifestyle that will allow you to eat well, and yet lose weight.

If you are going to fight fat, you have to have a winning plan. You have to work at it all the time, and once you reach your goal you must still remain faithful to your plan. It really is quite simple. Just know what number of calories you can eat and don't eat more than that number. The kind of food you eat does matter. You will need to make sure you maintain a balanced diet. It is strongly recommended that you eat at least 50 percent complex carbohydrates (such as potatoes, pasta, cereals with plenty of dietary fiber, and rice). It is also recommended that you severely limit saturated fats. Almost everyone agrees that drinking plenty of water is important. Water helps to rid your system of impurities and salts. Plus, drinking cold water forces your body to burn calories in order to raise the temperature of the water to body temperature, an added bonus. Be sure to start some exercise program under close medical supervision. Exercise is one of the key agents to increasing body metabolism, a must if you are going to continue losing weight.

Watch your calories and you will be well on your way to success. This book is not intended to be the final answer to weight loss. Nor is it intended to be a "diet" book. It is intended to be a help in preparing excellent meals that are delicious but low in calories. The book will also give you carbohydrate, fat, cholesterol, protein, and fiber counts. They are intended to assist those who need the information. The aim of the book is to provide low-calorie recipes. All of the information given is approximate. Great care was taken to make the information as accurate as possible, but information can vary somewhat and the total count should be taken as being a close approximation.

Remember, it takes about 3,600 calories to gain or lose a pound of fat. What goes in, comes out. If you eat 3,600 extra calories you will get an additional pound of weight. If you cut back by 3,600 calories, you will lose one pound of weight. The choice is clear and the choice remains yours. You can try to argue that some people can eat more than others, but that does not do anything to help you lose the weight you are seeking to lose or maintain a certain weight. Set your goal, see your doctor, exercise, and COUNT YOUR CALORIES. Count them every day—every meal, every snack, and every bite of food you put into your mouth. You will succeed, because calories do count!

Substitutions

I wrote these recipes to my taste and with the intent to be low in calories. However, I realize this cookbook, or any cookbook for that matter, cannot meet all the needs of every individual. Please feel free to make the substitutions necessary to meet the special needs of your diet.

If you must cut out cholesterol, feel free to substitute margarine or diet margarine in every case that butter is specified. If margarine is called for, you can use diet margarine if you choose. Just remember, taste will change and so will texture, but not to the point of destroying the dish. If you can't have butter, then don't use it. When whole eggs are called for, you can use the cholesterol-free egg substitute (about 1/4 cup of liquid egg substitute per whole egg). Be sure to read the label on the egg substitute: some of them cut cholesterol, but add many more calories. In fact, it is always a good idea to read the labels of any product you use; you may find the bargain you are getting is no bargain at all.

I use a good deal of "Butter Buds" throughout the book in various recipes. It is a product you will find in the diet section of your supermarket and is readily available nationally. It is real butter that has been freeze-dried with the fat content removed. It is an excellent way of adding the butter taste back into your dishes. It has no fat and no cholesterol content per serving, which makes it a real asset in cooking. Butter Buds contain 12 calories per fluid once, compared to 200 calories per ounce in butter or margarine. Quite a savings! The product may have more sodium content than persons on a very low-sodium intake are allowed. It contains 170 mg of sodium per liquid ounce or 1/8 ounce dry. If that is more sodium than you are allowed or than you like, you can substitute artificial butter seasoning for the Butter Buds. Just season with the artificial butter (make sure it is not the salted one; you just want the butter flavor) to taste. The taste will be similar to the taste you will get with the Butter Buds, and it's certainly worth using if you have to restrict the intake of sodium. Remember, almost no substitution is as good as the original product, but for those of us who must make changes to be able to enjoy our food and still remain healthy, it is wonderful to be able to approximate the taste we are seeking.

If you have to restrict your intake of salt, feel free to use whatever salt substitute you have become accustomed to when preparing your meals. The same goes for sugar substitutes. Use what you are already using; you will be more familiar with the product. Remember not to cook with the sugar substitute "Equal." It will lose its sweet taste completely in the cooking process. You can sweeten with Equal after a product is heated or cooked, with excellent success.

Finally, if I haven't listed any substitute that you must make in your daily regimen, feel free to make that change in the recipes in this book. Don't skip a recipe because it has something in it you can't eat or simply don't like to eat. Prepare the recipe with the change needed and write your evaluation in the margin by the recipe. You will find all kinds of new possibilities will open up to you when you experiment with recipes according to your likes, dislikes, and individual dietary needs.

NOTE: For all recipes, carbohydrate, fat, protein, and fiber values are given in grams; cholesterol values are given in milligrams. "Trace" indicates a negligible amount of that item. The values are for one serving, unless otherwise indicated.

NEW AMERICAN LIGHT CUISINE

Breakfast

Breakfast is the most important meal of the day! I know all of you believe that with all your heart and soul. Well, maybe two or three of you do, assuming mostly overweight people are reading this book. The problem with overweight people is mainly that we have a preconceived set of rules we operate by. I call them the "I nevers." You know, "I never" eat breakfast because . . . It really doesn't matter what the reason is; we follow the rule no matter what. "I never" (at least until last year) ate breakfast. I would rather take the extra time for sleeping or watching the morning news show or any number of other reasons. I always heard that "breakfast is the most important meal of the day" but it didn't make any sense to me. You know, every calorie you eat adds up no matter when you eat it. Well, I found out it does matter how and when you eat the calories.

Breakfast is important because it starts the metabolism running. Our bodies are such fine-tuned pieces of machinery that they are programmed to run slowly until they can tell how much fuel they will obtain. They measure that early in the morning when we arise. If you skip breakfast, you are telling the computer in your brain to slow things down, because there won't be much fuel for the day. Instead of burning calories, you are working to conserve as many calories as possible.

So breakfast is important! It will get your metabolism going. I have tried to eat between 200 to 300 of my daily calories at breakfast. Guess what? After about three weeks, I got up starving for breakfast. Now "I never" skip breakfast! We have to use all that modern science can offer to help us to reduce and stay reduced.

I am only giving you a few suggestions for breakfast foods, because there are so many cereals, fruits, light breads, and prepared low-calorie breakfast foods that taste great and are easy to fix. I do like to start the day with some type of fiber and some type of fruit. I also drink a glass (8 ounces) of skim milk on most days. In the past, when I would diet, I'd have a large glass of fruit juice and skip the milk and think I was doing great. Well, skim milk by the glass is only 90 calories and orange juice by the glass is about 112. So I wasn't saving at all! It is better for you to have the fresh fruit and the milk and skip the juice. Tomato juice is the exception to this rule. It is great-tasting and also low in calories. You can have a glass for about 41 calories. That makes tomato juice a nice afternoon juice snack.

The bottom line is, eat breakfast. Just try it a few weeks and you'll soon see you will love it and you will feel better for it. It doesn't matter what you eat. Just write down the total caloric intake for the meal and keep the running total for the day. Be creative at breakfast time. Don't get stuck in the rut of eating the same thing every day. Change often; it will help you keep your interest in your breakfast.

The following recipes are just a few you may add to your breakfast planning. I do not intend them to be the only choices for your meal. They are meant to supplement and suggest. Remember . . . EAT BREAKFAST!

CREPE RECIPE

1 1/4 cup all-purpose flour
1/2 tsp. salt
1 tsp. sugar
1/8 tsp. orange peel spice
3 large eggs, lightly beaten

2 cups skim milk
2 tsp. melted butter,
** unsalted**
melted butter to brush
** crêpe pan**

Mix together dry ingredients with a wire whisk. Mix eggs with flour mixture by beating with a wire whisk until blended. Add the milk and 2 teaspoons of melted butter. Mix together well, then cover with plastic wrap and refrigerate for at least 2 hours.

When you are ready to make the crêpes, brush the bottom of the crêpe pan with a little melted butter and set over low heat. Pour in about 1/4 cup of batter at a time and tilt it all around to cover the entire bottom of the pan. Cook quickly until the bottom is lightly browned; turn over and just lightly cook the other side. Repeat the process until all the crêpe batter is used. Let crêpes cool completely. Lay crêpes on top of each other and cover if you are going to store. Makes about 12 crêpes.

Lagniappe: This is an easy crêpe recipe and you can use it any time you
are in need of a crêpe recipe. It may be made in advance and
refrigerated or frozen for later use. Be sure you allow the crêpes to
cool completely before you cover them or they will stick or become
soggy. I like to cover them with plastic wrap because it does not
allow odors from the refrigerator or freezer to mingle with the crêpes
and ruin the taste.

*PER CREPE: Calories — 86; Carb — 2.6; Fat — 2.2; Chol — 73.5; Pro —
4.1; Fib — Trace*

WHOLE WHEAT PANCAKES

2 large eggs, slightly
  beaten
1 cup skim milk
1/2 tsp. vanilla extract
2/3 cup whole wheat flour,
  sifted
1/3 cup all-purpose flour

1/2 tsp. baking powder
1/4 tsp. baking soda
1/2 tsp. salt
1 tbsp. sugar
1/2 tsp. nutmeg
vegetable oil spray

In a mixing bowl, add the eggs, skim milk, and vanilla; blend well together. In a small bowl, mix together all the remaining ingredients except for the vegetable oil spray until well blended. Slowly beat the egg mixture into the flour mixture, but do not over-stir or it will make the pancakes tough.

Spray a nonstick skillet with the vegetable oil spray and heat over low heat. Spoon about 1/3 cup of batter into the hot skillet; tilt the skillet a little to let the pancake spread out. Cook over the low heat until the top of the cake becomes firm enough for you to turn it (it should be lightly browned on the bottom). Cook the other side for about 30 seconds or until it is just lightly brown. Serve right from the skillet. Serves 6.

Lagniappe: This batter can be made a few hours in advance and refrigerated until you are ready to use, if necessary. The pancakes will, however, rise more if the batter is freshly made. You can make the pancakes completely, tightly wrap when they are cool, and freeze for later use. They freeze very well. To reheat, thaw in the refrigerator and just add them back to a warm skillet and heat up on both sides until they are warm. Use diet margarine and diet syrup or sprinkle lightly with powdered sugar. I like them just plain or with a teaspoon of preserves.

Calories—122; Carb—18.7; Fat—2.4; Chol—92.0; Pro—5.9; Fib—0.4

PAIN PERDU
(French Toast)

1/2 tsp. nutmeg
1/2 tsp. cinnamon
1/4 tsp. ginger
1/8 tsp. cloves
2 tbsp. sugar
2 large eggs, well beaten
1/2 tsp. vanilla extract

2 tbsp. water
6 slices light bread, stale if
   possible (40 calories per
   slice)
vegetable oil spray
2 tsp. powdered sugar

In a small bowl, mix together the nutmeg, cinnamon, ginger, cloves, and sugar. Add the vanilla and water to the eggs and beat in for 30 seconds. Add the mixed spices and beat them in well. Take the bread and dip it into the egg batter to coat both sides.

Heat a large heavy skillet over low heat. When it is hot remove it from the heat and spray it lightly with the vegetable oil spray. Return to the heat and fry each slice of egg-battered bread until lightly browned on both sides. Sprinkle with 1/3 teaspoon of powdered sugar. Serve at once. Makes 6 slices of French toast and can serve 3 to 4 people.

Lagniappe: This is a simple and quick breakfast fare. Don't do anything in advance, except for letting your bread go stale. It is fast and clean-up is also a breeze. If someone wants the bread a little sweeter, just sprinkle on a packet of Equal sweetener with the powdered sugar and it will be very sweet.

PER SLICE OF TOAST: Calories — 62; Carb — 12.7; Fat — 2.1; Chol — 91.4; Pro — 4.1; Fib — Trace

HAM AND CHEESE OMELET

2 large eggs, beaten
1 tbsp. water
1 tsp. Butter Buds
1/8 tsp. Tabasco sauce
1/4 tsp. Worcestershire
  sauce
1/4 tsp. garlic powder
1/4 tsp. salt

1/8 tsp. nutmeg
vegetable oil spray
1 slice reduced calorie
  Swiss flavored cheese
1/4 packet wafer-thin
  sliced ham (the packet
  should be 2 1/2 oz.)

Beat together all the ingredients but the last three for 1 minute with a wire whisk. Heat a medium skillet or an omelet pan over medium heat until hot. Remove from the heat and spray with the vegetable oil spray. Return to the heat and put the egg mixture into the pan. Tilt the pan around to let the egg spread. Gently lift the edges of the egg to help solidify the edges. Chop the cheese and the ham together and sprinkle around the omelet just before the center sets. Fold the omelet out onto a warm serving plate. Serve at once. Serves 1.

Lagniappe: This is a quick ham and cheese omelet. It is great for breakfast or as an entree for dinner or lunch. Make it just before you are ready to eat. You can multiply this recipe by the number you are serving. I like to make one at a time so I can be exact on the measurements to control calories accurately.

Calories — 259; Carb — 4.1; Fat — 18.0; Chol — 551.0; Pro — 23.2; Fib — Trace

MUSHROOM OMELET

vegetable oil spray
2 tsp. diet margarine
6 large mushrooms, sliced
1/4 tsp. green onions,
    chopped
1 tsp. Butter Buds
1/4 tsp. salt
1/4 tsp. white pepper
4 large eggs, beaten

2 tbsp. water
1/8 tsp. Tabasco sauce
1/8 tsp. nutmeg
1/4 tsp. salt
1/4 tsp. onion powder
fresh parsley, minced for
    garnish
paprika for garnish

Heat a medium sauté pan over medium heat until it is hot; remove it from the heat, spray with the vegetable oil spray, and return to the heat. Add the diet margarine and let it melt. When the margarine begins to smoke, add the mushrooms and green onions and sauté for 3 minutes. Sprinkle with the dry Butter Buds and salt, then remove from the heat and set aside for later use.

Heat a medium skillet or omelet pan over medium heat until hot, remove from the heat, and lower the temperature to low. Spray with the vegetable oil spray and return to the heat. Beat together the remaining ingredients except for the last two until well mixed. Pour half of the mixture into the skillet; the omelet will begin to set at the edges. Spoon half of the mushroom mixture into the center of the omelet. Tilt the skillet, lift one half of the omelet, and fold over almost directly in half (just leave a little overhang). Cook for 30 seconds, then carefully flip over and cook for 30 more seconds. Slide the omelet onto a warm plate and set aside while the other omelet is cooked. Repeat the entire process for the other omelet. Garnish both omelets lightly with fresh parsley and paprika. Serve at once. Serves 2.

Lagniappe: An omelet needs to be eaten right after it has been cooked. You can prepare everything in advance and just cook the omelet when you are ready to eat. I have tried freezing an omelet; it does freeze and holds nicely, but the egg picks up freezer burn very easily and also "freezer taste." The cooking time is such that it really does make sense to cook just before eating. I have this omelet in the breakfast section, but it can certainly be eaten as a main course. You can also use this recipe and change the filling to suit your tastes. You can also substitute 1 cup of liquid egg substitute for the eggs if you are watching your cholesterol. In fact, any time eggs are called for, you can substitute 1/4 cup of liquid egg substitute for each egg.

Calories — 198; Carb — 5.9; Fat — 18.0; Chol — 548.0; Pro — 13.7; Fib — 0.5

INSTANT OATMEAL BREAKFAST

1/2 cup boiling water
1 packet instant oatmeal,
   flavor of your choice

1 tsp. Butter Buds
1 packet Equal sweetener
1/8 tsp. orange peel spice

Mix together the boiling water and the oatmeal. Stir well. Add the Butter Buds and blend in. Add the Equal and orange peel spice. Stir and eat at once. Serves 1.

Lagniappe: This is a quick and delicious breakfast. I eat it so often for breakfast that I decided it needed to be in this book. The Butter Buds really make it! It gives it the rich taste of real butter without the calories. The Equal sweetens it enough to make it really enjoyable!

Calories — 186; Carb — 38.0; Fat — 2.0; Chol — 1.9; Pro — 5.0; Fib — 0.4

HOMEMADE BREAKFAST SAUSAGE

1/2 lb. very lean pork,
  ground
1 lb. fresh white turkey
  meat, ground
1 1/2 tsp. salt
1/2 tsp. cayenne pepper
1/2 tsp. sage

1/8 tsp. cumin
1/4 tsp. paprika
1/4 tsp. white pepper
1/8 tsp. thyme
1/4 tsp. sweet basil
1/4 cup crushed ice
vegetable oil spray

Using your hands, blend together the pork and turkey meat until well mixed. Mix together all the seasonings and season evenly the ground meats. Work in the crushed ice and shape into 12 large breakfast patties. Heat a large skillet that has been lightly sprayed with the vegetable oil spray over medium heat and fry the sausage until well browned on both sides. Or you can broil the sausage, without using any vegetable oil spray, in the oven about 4 inches from the broiler. Be sure to cook pork well. Makes 12 patties.

Lagniappe: These patties are good when made in advance and refrigerated or frozen for later use. I put wax paper between each patty and wrap about 4 to 6 together in one freezer bag. You can also wrap them individually in plastic wrap and freeze. This is a way to get the breakfast sausage taste without the calories, fat, or cholesterol.

Calories — 124; Carb — 0.2; Fat — 5.5; Chol — 42.3; Pro — 18.4; Fib — Trace

Appetizers

Just because you are trying to lose weight doesn't mean life has to be dull! Be sure to include a few appetizers each week to brighten up your menus and make them more interesting. Keep the appetizers low in calories but high in taste, texture, and appearance. It is very important that you don't let your meals become plain, because there is a danger you'll go looking around and end up having a high-calorie dish.

Don't make the mistake of thinking empty calories are just fine because empty means "0" calories. Empty calories mean high calories with no corresponding food value. I'm not saying you can never have a totally wasted empty calorie, but just be sure you have the calories left for the day and it is really what you want to spend your calories on. My daughter comes to mind as an example of the point I want to make. She gets an allowance and therefore often has a bit of change built up. We might be shopping at a department store and she will see something she says she really wants.

"I'd do anything to have this or that," she might say. "It is my favorite thing in the whole world and it only costs $1.49. Can I please have it, please?"

I can always tell if she really wants something or not by what she is willing to pay for it. If she really wants something, then she will gladly spend her money for it. If she only has a fleeting interest, she is not about to spend money for it. If there is a point to be made in all this, it is this: don't spend your calories on anything you really don't want, but do make yourself have interesting choices that will add zest to your meals and offer a lot of variety.

Appetizers can be an important addition to your menu planning, lifting any meal from the mundane into the sublime. Experiment and enjoy!

ASPARAGUS ROLL-UPS

16 slices light whole wheat
    bread (40 calories per
    slice)
1/4 cup diet margarine
1/2 tsp. shallots, minced
2 cloves garlic, minced
2 tsp. fresh parsley,
    minced
1/8 tsp. Tabasco sauce

1 tsp. Butter Buds
2 tbsp. Romano cheese,
    grated
16 whole asparagus
    spears, drained and pat-
    ted dry with paper
    towels
vegetable oil spray

Preheat the oven to 275 degrees. Trim the crusts off the bread. Place the bread between two pieces of plastic wrap and use a rolling pin to roll the bread flat. In a sauce pan over medium heat, melt the margarine. When the margarine begins to smoke, add the shallots, garlic, and parsley and sauté for 3 minutes. Add the Tabasco sauce and Butter Buds and mix in well. Use a pastry brush and brush the slices of bread with the seasoned margarine, then sprinkle with a little Romano cheese. Place an asparagus spear near one point of bread and roll up like a jelly roll. Place on a baking sheet lightly sprayed with the vegetable oil spray. Bake at 275 degrees until the roll-ups are lightly brown. Serve hot. Serves 8.

Lagniappe: These roll-ups may be made in advance and frozen unbaked or refrigerated unbaked to be used at a later time. To use, just thaw in the refrigerator and bake as above. This is a somewhat different appetizer. It is simple to make and you can store a few servings in the freezer for those unexpected dinner guests. They make nice appetizers or just something unique to nibble on.

Calories — 134; Carb — 16.7; Fat — 4.1; Chol — 3.6; Pro — 7.1; Fib — 2.3

OYSTER-CASHEW MOLD

2 packages unflavored
  gelatin
1/2 cup cold water
1 can cream of mushroom
  soup
1 package (8 oz.) light
  cream cheese, chopped
  into squares
1 pt. fresh oysters with
  their liquid
1/2 cup cashews, chopped
1/4 tsp. salt

1/4 tsp. white pepper
1/2 tsp. Tabasco sauce
1/2 tsp. garlic powder
1/4 tsp. sweet basil
1 tsp. paprika
1 tbsp. white Worces-
  tershire sauce
1/4 cup green onions,
  minced
1 tbsp. fresh parsley,
  minced
fresh parsley for garnish

Add the unflavored gelatin to the cold water and stir well until it is dissolved. Heat the mushroom soup in a saucepan over medium heat until it reaches the bubbling point, then add the light cream cheese. In another small saucepan over medium heat, add the oysters and their liquid. Let the liquid come to a simmer, taking care to gently stir the oysters. Simmer for about 2 minutes or until the oysters become puffy and somewhat white in color. Remove from the heat and let them cool in the liquid. The cream cheese should be melted in the mushroom soup by this time, so add all the remaining ingredients and stir them in well. Remove from the heat.

When the oysters are cool enough to touch, chop them into bite-size pieces (about into fourths for large oysters) and put them into the seasoned soup mixture. Stir them through. Pour into a gelatin mold, cover with plastic wrap, and refrigerate until the gelatin is firmly set. When you are ready to serve, unmold onto a plate and garnish with fresh parsley. Serve with crackers. Serves 12.

Lagniappe: This is an easy dish that can be made up to 48 hours in advance for later use. It is excellent as a light appetizer, and also does well as a dish to bring to a party. If you have trouble unmolding this or any other gelatin mold, just put a little warm water in the bottom of your kitchen sink about 1 inch below the level of the gelatin mold. Place the mold in the warm water for 10 seconds, lift out, dry the water off the mold bottom, and unmold on a plate. Do not freeze this dish.

If you are not watching calories, you can make this with regular cream cheese for a richer taste.

Calories — 123; Carb — 5.7; Fat — 8.6; Chol — 97.1; Pro — 6.7; Fib — 0.2

AMY LOU'S CHICKEN
LIVER SPECIAL

1 lb. chicken livers	1/4 tsp. cayenne pepper
2 tbsp. diet margarine	1/4 cup green onions,
1 clove garlic, minced	chopped
1 tsp. shallots, minced	1/4 tsp. fresh parsley,
2 tsp. Butter Buds	minced
1/2 tsp. salt	1/4 tsp. Tabasco sauce
1/2 tsp. white pepper	1/2 cup dry vermouth

Wash the chicken livers and pat dry with paper towels. In a heavy skillet over medium-high heat, melt the margarine. When the margarine begins to smoke, not brown, add the chicken livers, garlic, and shallots. Sauté until the livers brown, about 4 minutes. Add the Butter Buds, salt, peppers, green onions, and parsley; sauté for 2 more minutes. Add the Tabasco sauce and vermouth; reduce the heat to simmer and simmer 10 minutes. Serve either over a hot plate or in a chafing dish. Use toothpicks as serving helpers. Serves 8.

Lagniappe: This recipe can be made in advance and refrigerated for later use. Do not keep for more than 24 hours refrigerated, as chicken livers tend to spoil easily. Do not freeze this dish; it will break the livers apart and will look terrible. You can also serve this dish as an entree for four.

Calories — 123; Carb — 1.5; Fat — 4.7; Chol — 360.6; Pro — 14.1; Fib — 0.1

BLUE CHEESE DIP
FOR VEGETABLES

1 sprig fresh parsley
2 cloves garlic, cut in half
1 package light cream
   cheese
1/4 cup skim milk
3 tbsp. light mayonnaise

1 tbsp. white Worces-
   tershire sauce
1/4 tsp. Tabasco sauce
1/4 tsp. dry hot mustard
1 tbsp. blue cheese,
   crumbled

Put the parsley and garlic in a food processor and blend at high speed until minced. Add the cream cheese and all the remaining ingredients except for the blue cheese. Mix together until smooth and creamy. Pour into a mixing bowl and fold in the blue cheese crumbles. Refrigerate for at least 4 hours before serving. Serve with plenty of fresh vegetables. This is an excellent dipping sauce for vegetables, even if you aren't concerned with watching calories. Serves 12.

Lagniappe: You can make this dip in advance, up to 4 days, and keep in the refrigerator. The longer it stays, the more blue cheese flavor it will absorb.

If you are not counting calories, this is great with corn chips.

Calories — 66; Carb — 3.4; Fat — 6.0; Chol — 21.7; Pro — 2.4; Fib — Trace

DAVE'S DILL DIP

1/2 cup yogurt, low-fat
1/2 cup light mayonnaise
1 1/2 tbsp. green onions,
   minced
1 tbsp. fresh parsley,
   minced
1 tbsp. fresh spinach,
   minced

1 tsp. Beau Monde
   seasoning
1/4 tsp. Tabasco sauce
1 tsp. Worcestershire
   sauce
1 tsp. dill
fresh raw vegetables cut
   for dipping

Mix all ingredients together, except for the raw cut vegetables, and blend well. Refrigerate for at least 10 hours to allow the flavors to mix. Serve with fresh raw vegetables. Makes just a little over 1 cup of dip. Serves 12.

Lagniappe: This dip can be made up to 2 days in advance. It is a light, fresh dip for raw vegetables. Use it with your choice of raw vegetables. I like to cut the vegetables into different shapes and use at least 4 different colors to add to the ambience of the dish.

Calories — 42; Carb — 0.6; Fat — 3.5; Chol — 0.6; Pro — 1.2; Fib — 0.1

MARINATED MUSHROOMS

1 1/2 lb. mushrooms, small
1/4 cup olive oil
2 tbsp. corn oil
2 cups red wine vinegar
3 cloves garlic, minced
1 medium onion, sliced
1 tbsp. fresh ground black pepper

3 packets Equal sweetener
1/2 tsp. Tabasco sauce
2 tbsp. Worcestershire sauce
1/2 tsp. celery seeds
3 whole cloves
2 whole allspice
1/4 cup bell pepper, diced

Wash the mushrooms. Cut off any bad pieces. Mix together well all ingredients in a large bowl. Pour into a large glass jar or crock and refrigerate for 3 days. Serve chilled. Serves 15.

Lagniappe: This is a recipe you have to make ahead. You can even store it for up to 1 week. It is great for parties and as a first course before dinner. Try to find nice white mushrooms on the first day the store puts them out; they will last better and have fewer marks on them.

Calories — 53; Carb — 3.5; Fat — 5.7; Chol — Trace; Pro — 1.1; Fib — 0.4

COCKTAIL VEAL MEATBALLS

1 1/2 lb. ground veal
3 whole rice cakes,
  crumbled
1 medium onion, minced
2 cloves garlic, minced
1/4 cup celery, minced
1/4 cup bell pepper,
  minced
1/4 tsp. Tabasco sauce
1 tsp. salt
1/4 tsp. sweet basil
1/4 tsp. oregano
1/4 tsp. rosemary
1 tbsp. fresh parsley,
  minced

1 tbsp. Worcestershire
  sauce
1 large egg, slightly beaten
vegetable oil spray
1 cup reduced calorie chili
  sauce
1/2 cup reduced calorie
  catsup
1/2 cup low-calorie grape
  jelly (not made with
  Equal sweetener)
3 tbsp. fresh lemon juice
1/4 cup green onion tops,
  chopped
2 tbsp. honey

In a large mixing bowl, mix all but the last seven ingredients together until well blended. Roll the mixture into about 72 small meatballs. Heat a large, heavy nonstick skillet over medium heat. When it is hot, remove from the heat and spray it lightly with the vegetable oil spray. Brown the meatballs about one-third at a time until they are all browned. Return them to the skillet and add the chili sauce, catsup, grape jelly, lemon juice, green onion tops, and honey. Bring to a simmer and let simmer for 45 minutes. Serve hot with toothpicks. This is an appetizer or party food. Serves 12.

Lagniappe: This recipe can be made completely in advance and refrigerated or frozen for later use. When I am going to freeze or refrigerate, I like to simmer the sauce for only 30 minutes, then cool to freeze or refrigerate. When ready to serve, simply thaw in the refrigerator, return to a saucepan over medium heat, and bring to a simmer. Reduce the heat and simmer for 15 minutes.

You can have a lot of fun with this recipe. You can add pineapple chunks and bell pepper strips to it and call it **Meatballs Hawaiian.** This is a great recipe to "play" with, so have at it.

Calories — 250; Carb — 19.2; Fat — 15.1; Chol — 74.3; Pro — 14.5; Fib — 0.2

SHRIMP DIP

1 sprig fresh parsley	**3 tbsp. light mayonnaise**
1 tsp. shallots, minced	**1 lb. boiled shrimp, peeled**
1 package light cream	**and deveined and**
cheese	**chopped**
1/4 cup skim milk	**1/2 tsp. sweet basil**
2 tbsp. white Worces-	**1/2 tsp. Tabasco sauce**
tershire sauce	**1/4 tsp. dry hot mustard**

Put the parsley and shallots into a food processor and blend at high speed until minced. Add the cream cheese, skim milk, light mayonnaise, and Worcestershire sauce. Mix together until smooth and creamy. Pour into a mixing bowl, add the boiled, chopped shrimp and the remaining ingredients, and fold in well.

Refrigerate for at least 3 hours before serving. Serve with plenty of fresh vegetables cut into "chips" or serve with toast points made from light bread. This is an excellent dip for almost any kind of dipping "chip." If you have to worry about calories, corn chips and any cracker are also excellent. Serves 30.

Lagniappe: You can make this dip in advance, up to 24 hours, and keep in the refrigerator. This is a cooked seafood dip, so be sure to keep it well refrigerated and try not to keep it for longer than 2 days. This is also an excellent dip to bring anytime you are responsible for bringing a dip; no one will have to know that it is a low-calorie dip!

Calories — 40; Carb — 1.7; Fat — 2.6; Chol — 31.2; Pro — 3.7; Fib — Trace

CUCUMBER SPREAD

2 large cucumbers
1/2 cup onions, minced
2 tbsp. green onions,
   minced
1 package (8 oz.) light
   cream cheese

2 tbsp. light mayonnaise
1/4 tsp. Tabasco sauce
1/4 tsp. garlic powder
1/2 tsp. salt
1 tsp. fresh lemon juice
1 tsp. red wine vinegar

Wash the cucumbers well and dry with a paper towel. Cut off both ends, and grate both cucumbers completely, leaving the skin on. Use a cheesecloth and put the grated cucumbers in the center. Close the cloth around the cucumbers and squeeze out as much liquid as possible. Mix well the cucumbers with the onions and green onions.

In a food processor (or using an electric mixer), beat the cream cheese until smooth. Add the remaining ingredients and blend together thoroughly. Add the cucumber mixture and blend again until smooth. Allow the mixture to chill for about 1 hour in the refrigerator. Serve as a spread with raw vegetables or low-calorie crackers. Makes about 2 cups.

Lagniappe: You can make this spread in advance and store in the refrigerator for up to one week. Just whip it a little before serving. It is an excellent snack before dinner and a really nice party food. Do not freeze. For variety you can add crabmeat or shrimp to this dip and change it completely. I also like to open a can of smoked oysters, chop them well, and blend into this spread for a wonderful smoked flavor.

PER CUP: Calories — 352; Carb — 10.9; Fat — 31.9; Chol — 124.0; Pro — 10.7; Fib — 1.0

Soups

Often, the soup section of a cookbook is overlooked. In a low-calorie cookbook, I feel the reader should take a long hard look at the soup recipes, then move even further and try using soups to lower a meal's caloric intake and yet offer full satisfaction. Soups make excellent light lunches or dinners. They also can be used to cut an appetite during the morning or evening. This gives them a strong position in helping to lower overall caloric intake.

Try looking at and then using a few of the soup recipes given in this book. Make them just as I have, and then make notes in the margin about your likes and dislikes. Try some of the changes offered in the lagniappe section. The important point is to broaden your tastes by trying something new. My daughter has a friend who hardly eats anything. Her likes in food can be counted on one hand. Sometimes I get her to try something just a little different and it becomes her favorite food once she has tried it. I'm having no luck with squash, but I think the point is clear. Until we have made something new and given it a fair trial, we really might be missing out on quite a lot.

Soups can broaden your menus without adding great quantities of calories. Experiment with some of the soups within! I hope one or two become your new favorites.

GARLIC-BASIL SOUP

1 tbsp. olive oil, extra
  virgin
5 cloves garlic, minced
1 large bay leaf
1 tbsp. fresh basil,
  chopped
1 tsp. flour
1/8 tsp. Tabasco sauce
1 qt. beef stock or beef
  broth, simmering hot

salt and fresh ground
  black pepper to taste
1/8 tsp. white pepper
1/4 tsp. garlic powder
2 large egg yolks, lightly
  beaten
1 tbsp. fresh parsley,
  minced
4 thin slices French bread,
  toasted

In a sauté pan over medium-high heat, bring the olive oil to the smoking point. Add the garlic and bay leaf and sauté until the garlic is brown, stirring constantly. Add the basil and sauté for 1 more minute. Add the flour and cook for 3 minutes, stirring. Add 1 cup of the beef stock and blend in well. Pour the garlic-stock mixture into a stockpot and add the rest of the beef stock. Place over medium heat and season to taste with salt and fresh ground black pepper. Add the Tabasco sauce, white pepper, and garlic powder. Bring to a low simmer and cook for 10 minutes.

Place the eggs in a small bowl and slowly add 1 cup of the soup mixture, beating the egg together with the soup. Pour the egg-stock mixture into the stockpot. Add the fresh parsley and stir in well. Place the French bread into each of four soup bowls and pour the soup over the bread. Serve at once. Serves 4.

Lagniappe: This is such an easy soup to make, don't do it in advance. The egg mixture makes it difficult to deal with if you do not serve it at once. Do not freeze this soup. If you are set on doing some of it in advance, just do up to the adding of the egg and refrigerate until you are ready to continue. This makes either a nice before-dinner soup or a light lunch selection.

Calories — 146; Carb — 15.4; Fat — 8.4; Chol — 136.0; Pro — 6.9; Fib — 0.5

TOMATO-YOGURT SOUP

2 cups canned tomatoes,
  chopped
1/4 cup onions, chopped
1 clove garlic, minced
1 stalk celery, chopped
1/2 cup yogurt, low-calorie

1/4 tsp. sweet basil leaves
1/4 cup fresh chives,
  minced
1 tbsp. fresh lime juice
1/8 tsp. Tabasco sauce
1/2 tsp. salt

Put the first four ingredients into a medium saucepan over medium heat and bring to a boil; turn down the heat to simmer. Let the mixture simmer for 5 minutes. Remove the mixture from the heat and chill for at least 1 hour. Strain the soup and chill until ready to serve.

When you are ready to serve, mix together the strained liquid and all other ingredients and blend together well. Serve chilled. Serves 4.

Lagniappe: This recipe may be made in advance and refrigerated for later use. Just do not mix together until you are ready to serve. Do not freeze; it will keep in the refrigerator for 3 or 4 days before serving without any decrease in flavor or quality. You may also serve this soup hot if you choose. Just heat the strained mixture to the boiling point over medium heat, then reduce the heat, add the remaining ingredients, mix, and bring to the serving temperature you desire. I like it both ways.

Calories — 54; Carb — 9.8; Fat — 0.7; Chol — 1.8; Pro — 3.2; Fib — 1.1

SOUP PARMESAN

1 qt. beef stock or beef
  broth
1/8 tsp. Tabasco sauce
4 slices French bread,
  toasted

1 tbsp. green onion tops,
  minced
1 tbsp. fresh parsley,
  minced
4 tbsp. Parmesan cheese

In a large saucepan over medium heat, bring the beef stock to a simmer. Add the Tabasco sauce and stir through. Add the green onions and parsley and heat for 1 minute. Put 1 slice of French bread toast into each of four soup bowls and pour the beef stock over them. Sprinkle the bread with 1 tablespoon of Parmesan cheese and serve at once. Serves 4.

Lagniappe: This soup is quite simple and is particularly excellent if you use homemade beef stock. You can and should make the stock well in advance, so the time spent in preparation of the soup itself is not long at all. This is a light but delicious soup.

Calories—112; Carb—13.3; Fat—3.0; Chol—4.0; Pro—7.3; Fib—Trace

NAVY BEAN SOUP

1 lb. dry navy beans, rinsed once
3 qt. cold water
3 qt. beef stock or beef broth
1 tsp. salt
1/2 tsp. cayenne pepper
1/4 tsp. Tabasco sauce
1/4 tsp. sweet basil
1 cup white onions, minced

1/4 cup sweet bell peppers, minced
1/4 cup celery, minced
2 cloves garlic, minced
1 can (10 3/4 oz.) Rotel tomatoes
1 cup green onions, chopped
1/2 cup fresh parsley, minced

Soak the navy beans overnight in the cold water. It should cover the beans completely. When finished soaking, drain and rinse the beans once. In a large stockpot over medium heat, add the beans and the remaining ingredients. Cook until the beans are tender, yet hold together. Serve hot. Serves 8.

Lagniappe: This is truly a vegetable stock soup. You do have beef stock, but the real flavor is the bean stock. It is very tempting and inexpensive. You can make this soup in advance and freeze or refrigerate until you are ready to serve. Just thaw in the refrigerator, return to the large stockpot, bring to a simmer, and serve.

Calories — 140; Carb — 10.1; Fat — 1.0; Chol — Trace; Pro — 6.7; Fib — 1.0

CHICKEN SOUP ORIENTAL

3 cups chicken stock or chicken broth
1 tbsp. soy sauce
1 tbsp. red wine vinegar
1 cup bok choy, chopped
1 cup broccoli, chopped
1/2 cup celery, cut diagonally in 1/2-inch pieces
1/2 cup carrots, julienned
1 cup fresh snow peas, cleaned

4 large mushrooms, sliced
1/8 tsp. fresh grated ginger
1/4 tsp. Tabasco sauce
1/2 tsp. salt
1/4 cup green onions, chopped
2 tbsp. parsley, minced
1 cup chicken breast, cooked and cut into bite-size pieces

Put the chicken stock, soy sauce, vinegar, bok choy, broccoli, celery, and carrots into a large saucepan over high heat and bring to a boil. Let boil for 1 minute, then reduce the heat to a simmer and add the remaining ingredients. Simmer for 5 to 7 minutes or until the vegetables are tender, but crisp. Serve hot. Makes 6 1-cup servings.

Lagniappe: This soup can be made in advance, but do not simmer for the whole time—only about 2 minutes—then remove from the heat and cool. When you are ready to serve, just return to heat and bring to a simmer for about 2 more minutes, then serve. You can freeze this soup without any problems. The vegetables are crisper if you serve right after cooking, but the taste, texture, and quality is still there if done in advance. This is a nice lunch or appetizer.

Calories — 67; Carb — 5.9; Fat — 0.8; Chol — 12.7; Pro — 9.1; Fib — 0.8

ONION SOUP

1 tbsp. butter or margarine
2 medium onions, chopped
2 tsp. flour
1 qt. beef stock or beef
  broth, simmering
1/8 tsp. Tabasco sauce
1/8 tsp. white pepper
1 tsp. salt

fresh ground black pepper
  to taste
4 slices French bread,
  toasted
1 tbsp. fresh parsley,
  minced
1 tbsp. Parmesan cheese
1 1/2 tbsp. Romano cheese

In a sauté pan, melt the butter over high heat. When the butter starts to smoke, add the onions and sauté over high heat, stirring constantly until the onions brown well. Reduce the heat to medium, add the flour, and blend it in well. Cook for 2 minutes, constantly stirring. Add 1 cup of the beef stock and blend it in well. Transfer the onion mixture to a stockpot and add the remaining stock, Tabasco sauce, white pepper, and black pepper. Simmer the soup for 7 minutes.

Put the slices of French bread into serving bowls and pour the hot soup over the bread. Sprinkle with the parsley. Mix together the Parmesan and Romano cheeses, then sprinkle over the bread. Serve at once. Serves 4.

Lagniappe: This is an easy onion soup, but the taste is quite good. If you use homemade beef stock it will be all the better. If you want to reduce the calories even more, you can substitute diet margarine for the butter, but you will be reducing flavor as well. This soup can be completely made up to pouring of the soup over the bread and either refrigerated or frozen. Freezing does tend to reduce the onion taste somewhat, but it is still quite good. To serve, just thaw in the refrigerator, bring to a simmer in a stockpot, and pick up the recipe at the pouring of the soup over the bread. This is a nice soup to serve as an appetizer or for lunch.

Calories — 170; Carb — 18.5; Fat — 4.9; Chol — 14.8; Pro — 10.1; Fib — 0.4

FRESH RHUBARB SOUP

1 large white onion, minced
2 cloves garlic, minced
3 tbsp. diet margarine
1 lb. rhubarb, trimmed and cut into 1/2-inch thick slices
1/2 lb. carrots, sliced 1/2-inch thick
1 cup celery, sliced 1/2-inch thick
1 qt. chicken stock or chicken broth
1/2 cup uncooked short grain white rice
1 can (6 oz.) tomato paste
1 tsp. sugar
1/4 tsp. sweet basil
1/8 tsp. nutmeg
1 tbsp. fresh parsley, minced
1 tsp. salt
1/4 tsp. Tabasco sauce
1/4 tsp. white pepper
1 cup low-fat milk

In a large saucepan over medium heat, sauté the onions and garlic in the margarine until the onions are clear, about 5 minutes. Add the rhubarb, carrots, and celery and sauté for 3 minutes, stirring often. Add the remaining ingredients except for the milk and mix in well. Bring to a boil, then reduce to simmer and let the soup simmer until the rice is cooked, about 20 minutes. Remove from the heat and let the soup cool.

Purée the soup in a blender or food processor until smooth. Return to the saucepan and add the milk. Bring the soup just up to a simmer, but do not let it boil. Serve hot. Serves 8.

Lagniappe: This soup can be made completely in advance and refrigerated for later use. It will keep for 3 days in the refrigerator. Do not freeze. Just reheat to surprise you and your guests.

Calories — 153; Carb — 23.9; Fat — 2.1; Chol — 2.8; Pro — 6.4; Fib — 1.3

FRESH ZUCCHINI SOUP

3 tbsp. diet margarine
2 medium yellow onions,
　chopped
2 cloves garlic, minced
1/2 cup celery, chopped
1/4 cup bell pepper,
　chopped
2 1/2 lb. fresh zucchini, cut
　into circles

1 large carrot, coarsely cut
1 can (10 3/4 oz.) Rotel
　tomatoes
3 cups chicken stock or
　chicken broth
3 tbsp. Swiss cheese,
　grated
2 tbsp. fresh parsley,
　minced

In a large saucepan over medium heat, melt the margarine. When the margarine begins to smoke, add the onions, garlic, celery, and bell pepper and sauté, constantly stirring, for 5 to 7 minutes or until the onions are soft and clear. Add the zucchini and carrot and sauté for 3 more minutes, stirring. Add the Rotel tomatoes and chicken stock and bring to a boil; reduce to simmer and cook for 20 minutes, or until the zucchini is very tender. Break up the zucchini and tomatoes with a slotted spoon; mash until there are no large pieces left.

Ladle the soup into six individual soup dishes and garnish each with 1/2 teaspoon of Swiss cheese and a teaspoon of fresh parsley. Serve hot. Serves 6.

Lagniappe: This soup lends itself well to advance preparation. Just do not garnish with the Swiss cheese or parsley until you are ready to serve. You can refrigerate or freeze this soup. To serve, just thaw in the refrigerator, bring to a simmer, and serve as above. This soup has a good stock that adds richness, yet is low in calories. To lower the calories even more, just leave out the Swiss cheese.

Calories — 145; Carb — 17.3; Fat — 6.0; Chol — 7.0; Pro — 7.2; Fib — 1.9

BROCCOLI-LEMON SOUP

1 medium lemon
1 lb. broccoli, washed and
   trimmed
4 green onions, washed
   and trimmed both ends
1 carrot, scraped and
   cleaned
1/2 medium turnip,
   washed and cut both
   ends

1 1/4 qt. chicken stock or
   chicken broth
2 tsp. fresh lemon juice
1/4 tsp. Tabasco Sauce
salt to taste
fresh ground black pepper
   to taste
1 tsp. fresh chives
1/3 cup fresh parsley,
   minced

Slice the lemon as thinly as possible for use as a garnish, then set it aside for later use. Remove the florets from the trimmed stems of broccoli; place the green onions, carrot, and turnip into the chicken stock and bring it to a boil. Reduce to a low simmer and simmer for 20 minutes. Remove the vegetables from the stock and process them in a food processor or blender until minced. Pour this chopped vegetable mixture back into the chicken stock. Bring to a low simmer for 20 minutes. Add the broccoli florets and lemon juice, then 4 of the thin lemon slices. Season with the Tabasco sauce, salt, and black pepper and simmer for 10 more minutes. Add the chives and parsley and simmer for 2 minutes. In a large soup cup, place at least 2 of the florets and 1 fresh uncooked thin lemon slice. Serve either hot or cold. Serves 8.

Lagniappe: This is an easy low-calorie soup. I prefer it served hot, but it is quite tasty cold. You can make it in advance and store in the refrigerator, but do not freeze this soup.

Calories—62; Carb—10.1; Fat—1.2; Chol—0.6; Pro—6.1; Fib—1.3

CRABMEAT AND CORN SOUP

1/4 cup butter, unsalted
1/4 cup onions, chopped
1 clove garlic, minced
1 1/2 tsp. celery, minced
2 1/4 tbsp. all-purpose
  flour
1/4 tsp. sweet basil leaves
4 cups fresh or frozen corn
1 cup chicken stock or
  chicken broth

3 cups skim milk
1/2 cup half-and-half
  cream
1 tsp. salt (or to taste)
1/2 tsp. white pepper
1/4 tsp. Tabasco sauce
1 lb. fresh lump crabmeat
  (or may use any quality
  frozen crabmeat)

In a large, heavy saucepot over medium heat, sauté the onions, garlic, and celery in the butter until the onions are clear and limp. Add the flour and basil and cook for 2 minutes, constantly stirring. Mince the corn in a food processor or blender and add it to the mixture. Cook for 5 minutes over low-medium heat. Remove the pot from the heat and add the skim milk, chicken stock, half-and-half, salt, white pepper, and Tabasco sauce. Return the soup to medium heat and bring the mixture just to the boiling point, but do not let it boil. Add the crabmeat and heat it through. Serve at once. Serves 8.

Lagniappe: This recipe may be made in advance and refrigerated for later use. Do not freeze. To reheat, just slowly heat it over medium heat; take special care not to let it boil. If you want this soup to be richer, you can make it with regular milk and substitute heavy whipping cream for half-and-half.

Calories — 264; Carb — 10.0; Fat — 5.3; Chol — 81.3; Pro — 17.5; Fib — 0.4

SQUASH SOUP

1 lb. tender young yellow
    squash, cut into circles
3 cups chicken stock or
    chicken broth
1/8 tsp. Tabasco sauce
1/8 tsp. nutmeg
1/4 tsp. white pepper

1 tsp. salt
1 tsp. sugar
1 tbsp. green onion tops,
    minced
1 tbsp. parsley, minced
1 cup milk

In a stockpot over medium heat, add the squash, chicken stock, Tabasco, and nutmeg, then bring to a low rolling boil. Let the mixture boil for 10 minutes, then remove from the heat and either mash the squash with a fork or cool, put into a food processor, and blend until well mixed. Return to the heat and bring back to a simmer, then add the remaining ingredients. Stir together well. Simmer slowly for 2 minutes, taking care not to boil the soup to keep the milk from scorching. Serve hot. Serves 4.

Lagniappe: This soup can be made completely in advance and either frozen or refrigerated. Just thaw in the refrigerator and put in a stockpot over low heat until the soup is heated through. This is another easy soup that will complement most meals or serve as a light lunch.

You can use the same recipe to make **Broccoli Soup, Zucchini Soup,** or **Asparagus Soup,** simply by adding 1 pound of the substituted vegetable. Try your own vegetable variation!

Calories—95; Carb—9.6; Fat—3.2; Chol—9.5; Pro—7.1; Fib—0.7

Salads and
Salad Dressings

Almost everyone knows salads are good for you, but we rarely stop to ask why. Salads provide the necessary roughage to aid in the digestive process. They are full of fiber, fiber that in most cases is low in calories. You can use fiber to fill you up but not "fill you out." If you eat a big salad before your dinner, you are less likely to eat something that may be higher in calories. Therefore, salads are a necessary part of any program to reduce caloric intake.

This section offers you a variety of excellent salads—salads that can be a meal in themselves or salads that serve as a complement to any meal. I did not intend this section to be a listing of all salad foods. Often, I just like a large bowl of lettuce with a very low-calorie dressing. Use one of the dressings within or one of the excellent low-calorie dressings available in the supermarket. Take the time to shop and try some of them. Once you find one you like, be sure to write down the name. At times they all look alike.

Read the lagniappe section under each recipe to determine whether or not the dressing or salad can be made in advance. This will help save time when you are ready to begin your menu planning.

Be sure to include at least one type of salad a day in your meal planning. Salads will go a long way toward insuring your success at weight loss.

HOT CHICKEN SALAD

2 tbsp. peanut oil
1 cup cabbage, shredded
1/2 cup purple cabbage,
  shredded
1 cup cauliflower florets
1/4 cup celery, chopped
1/4 cup carrots, thinly
  sliced
4 large mushrooms, sliced
3 cups baked chicken, cut
  into bite-size pieces

2 cups fresh spinach,
  shredded
2 tbsp. soy sauce
2 tbsp. red wine vinegar
1 tbsp. Dijon mustard
1 tsp. sugar
1/2 tsp. salt
1/4 tsp. Tabasco sauce
1/4 cup toasted slivered
  almonds

Heat a large skillet over medium heat until hot. Add the peanut oil and heat until it smokes. Add the cabbage, purple cabbage, and cauliflower florets; sauté for 3 minutes. Be sure to pour in all at once to prevent the oil from splattering. Add the celery, carrots, and mushrooms and sauté for 3 more minutes. Add the remaining ingredients and heat together while stirring constantly for 2 more minutes to allow the flavors to blend. Spoon onto a salad serving plate and serve at once. Serves 6.

Lagniappe: Never make this salad in advance! Get everything ready, but do not make until you are ready to serve. This dish can either be a salad to serve with dinner or a meal in itself.

You can also use 3 cups of cooked turkey instead of chicken to make **Hot Turkey Salad.** This salad is quick and good. It provides a nice change from the usual.

Calories — 165; Carb — 7.0; Fat — 8.6; Chol — 36.5; Pro — 17.4; Fib — 1.1

CUCUMBERS ALONE

2 large fresh cucumbers,
    must be tender
1/2 cup white vinegar
1/2 cup red wine vinegar
1 tsp. Tabasco sauce
1/2 tsp. black pepper

1 tsp. salt
2 tsp. fresh lime juice
1 tbsp. fresh parsley
1 tsp. garlic powder
1/2 tsp. onion powder

Wash the cucumbers well to remove as much of the oil or wax from their skins as possible. Peel one of the cucumbers and cut the ends off the other one. Use a fork and score the second cucumber by pulling the fork down the cucumber until all of the surface is scored. Slice cucumbers about 1/2-inch thick. Add the cucumbers to a large mixing bowl and pour in remaining ingredients. Mix together well and chill for 30 minutes. Serve chilled. Serves 2.

Lagniappe: This recipe will really get your attention at first bite. It is colorful and very tasty. It is best to eat right after 30 minutes' refrigeration, but you can leave it for longer if necessary. The only problem you will be faced with is the cucumbers will slowly lose their crispness. The taste will still be super!

Calories — 50; Carb — 13.1; Fat — 0.3; Chol — Trace; Pro — 1.5; Fib — 0.8

COLESLAW

1/2 cup light mayonnaise
1/4 cup plain yogurt,
    low-fat
1/4 cup buttermilk
2 tsp. sugar
2 tbsp. fresh lemon juice
1/4 tsp. Tabasco sauce
1 tsp. salt
1/4 tsp. onion powder

1/4 tsp. white pepper
1/4 tsp. garlic powder
1/2 tsp. celery seeds
3 cups green cabbage,
    shredded
1 cup purple cabbage,
    shredded
1/4 cup green onions,
    minced

In a large mixing bowl, combine all the ingredients except the cabbage and green onion. Mix well. Combine the cabbage and green onions with the dressing mixture and toss the cabbage to coat it all well. Cover the bowl tightly and refrigerate for 12 hours. It really needs to refrigerate for so long to blend together the flavors. Just before the slaw is served, mix it together well to be sure that the dressing is equally distributed. Serve chilled. Serves 6.

Lagniappe: You can't freeze coleslaw, but you can make it up to 3 days in advance and refrigerate until you are ready to serve. This actually improves the dish. The purple cabbage in this slaw sets a nice color contrast to many entrees.

Calories — 104; Carb — 8.4; Fat — 1.4; Chol — 1.0; Pro — 2.1; Fib — 0.7

DEB'S HAM SALAD

1 package (2 1/2 oz.)
wafer-thin sliced ham,
diced
2 tbsp. light mayonnaise
1/2 tbsp. yellow mustard
1/4 cup celery, finely diced

1 tbsp. green onions,
minced
1 small dill pickle, minced
1/2 tsp. onion powder
dash Tabasco sauce

Mix all ingredients together well. Chill in the refrigerator for at least 1 hour to allow the flavors to blend. Serve chilled. Serves 2.

Lagniappe: This ham salad can be made in advance and refrigerated for up to 3 days before serving. It makes excellent sandwiches or you can stuff an avocado or tomato with it. If you are going to make a sandwich, use the low-calorie bread (40 calories per slice) and your total sandwich will be under 200 calories. This is a tasty sandwich for very few calories. A ham salad stuffed tomato would have even fewer!

Calories — 124; Carb — 6.8; Fat — 9.0; Chol — 18.0; Pro — 6.8; Fib — 0.1

FRESH CAULIFLOWER SALAD

1 head cauliflower, cut
   into florets
cold water
1 tsp. salt
3 tbsp. light mayonnaise
2 tbsp. olive oil, extra
   virgin
2 tbsp. fresh lemon juice
1 clove garlic, minced
1 tbsp. green onions,
   minced
1 tsp. Dijon mustard

1/2 cup pimento, diced
1/4 cup ripe black olives,
   chopped
1/2 tsp. salt
1 tsp. red wine vinegar
1/4 tsp. Tabasco sauce
1/4 tsp. white pepper
1/4 cup fresh parsley,
   minced
lettuce for salad bed
paprika for garnish

Wash the cauliflower florets well and set in a colander. In a large pot over high heat, add the water and salt. Bring to a hard boil, then add the cauliflower. Cook for 2 minutes, then pour back into the colander and let cool.

Mix together well all the remaining ingredients, except for the parsley, lettuce, and paprika, in a large bowl. When the cauliflower florets are cool, toss them with the dressing, taking care to coat the florets well. Sprinkle the top with fresh parsley, cover, and refrigerate for 4 or more hours. When ready to serve, toss well mixing the parsley throughout. Serve chilled on a bed of lettuce and garnish lightly with paprika. Serves 6.

Lagniappe: As the directions indicate, you can make in advance and refrigerate. It will keep for up to 3 days in the refrigerator. Do not freeze. This is a light salad that has good color and surprising taste. Serve this salad as a light lunch entree or as a salad course for dinner.

Calories — 132; Carb — 7.4; Fat — 9.5; Chol — Trace; Pro — 3.2; Fib — 1.4

GREEN PEA SALAD

2 cans (17 oz. each) sweet
  peas
1 cup celery, diced
1 cup fresh tomato,
  skinned and diced
1/2 cup purple onion,
  diced
1/2 cup sweet green
  pepper, diced
1/4 cup sweet red bell
  pepper, diced
2 slices low-calorie
  American cheese, diced
2 rice cakes, broken into
  small pieces
1 large hard-boiled egg,
  chopped
1/2 cup light mayonnaise
1/2 tsp. salt
1/4 tsp. cayenne pepper
1/8 tsp. Tabasco sauce
1/4 tsp. sweet basil
1/2 tsp. garlic powder
1 tbsp. fresh lemon juice
1 tbsp. red wine vinegar
1 tbsp. Worcestershire
  sauce
1 tsp. paprika
3 tbsp. green onion tops,
  minced
2 tbsp. fresh parsley,
  minced
lettuce leaves for salad
  bed

Mix together all ingredients, except for the lettuce leaves, in a large mixing bowl and refrigerate for at least 4 hours. Serve chilled on a bed of lettuce leaves. Serves 8.

Lagniappe: This is an easy but tasty dish. It can be made up to 3 days in advance, but is best when eaten the same day it is made. Do not freeze.

If you are not counting calories or cholesterol, you can substitute 2 more eggs hard-boiled for the rice cakes. This will make the salad closer to usual style.

Calories — 170; Carb — 17.8; Fat — 7.8; Chol — 38.0; Pro — 6.9; Fib — 6.6

GREEN BEAN SALAD

1 can (17 oz.) green beans,
  drained
1/4 cup red wine vinegar
1 tbsp. tarragon vinegar
2 tbsp. cold water
1 tbsp. corn oil
1 clove garlic, minced
1 tsp. salt
1/2 tsp. black pepper
1/4 tsp. white pepper
1/8 tsp. Tabasco sauce

1/2 tsp. fresh oregano,
  minced or 1/4 tsp. dry
  leaves
1 tbsp. fresh parsley,
  minced
1 tsp. fresh basil, minced
  or 1/4 tsp. dry
1/8 tsp. fresh thyme or a
  pinch of dry
1 large bay leaf, crumbled

In a large mixing bowl, mix all ingredients together except the beans, using a whisk. Add the beans and toss to coat all beans. Cover tightly and refrigerate for at least 4 hours. Serve chilled either as a vegetable or as a salad. Serves 4.

Lagniappe: This salad can be made in advance and stored in the refrigerator for up to 3 days. It will not hurt the taste at all; in fact, it will be even more flavorful. Do not freeze. If you like sweet taste in bean salad, just use 1 or 2 packets of Equal sweetener. It works well and does not add many calories.

Calories — 54; Carb — 5.9; Fat — 3.6; Chol — Trace; Pro — 2.8; Fib — 1.8

JUST PLAIN EGG SALAD

4 large hard boiled eggs,
  chopped
3 tbsp. light mayonnaise
1 tbsp. yellow mustard
1/2 cup celery, finely diced
1 tbsp. green onions,
  minced

1 large dill pickle, minced
1/2 tsp. garlic powder
1/2 tsp. salt
1/2 tsp. onion powder
1/4 tsp. paprika
dash Tabasco sauce

Mix all ingredients together well. Chill in the refrigerator for at least 1 hour to allow the flavors to blend. Serve chilled. Serves 2.

Lagniappe: This egg salad can be made in advance and refrigerated for up to 2 days before serving. I like to serve the egg salad on a bed of shredded lettuce or with a slice of tomato and lettuce on a sandwich made with light bread (40 calories per slice). This egg salad still has the great egg salad taste, but its low-calorie ingredients take the calorie count down.

Calories — 252; Carb — 8.0; Fat — 19.4; Chol — 548.0; Pro — 14.3; Fib — 0.8

CARROT-APPLE AMBROSIA

3 1/2 cups carrots, shredded
1 1/2 cups red apple, shredded with peel on
1/4 cup fresh lemon juice
1/3 cup coconut, dried shredded sweetened
1 cup miniature marshmallows
1/2 tsp. orange rind, take care not to get white
1 cup orange sections, chopped
1/2 cup lemon yogurt, low-fat
1/4 cup light mayonnaise
2 tbsp. honey
lettuce leaves for salad bed

In a large mixing bowl, toss the carrots and apple with the lemon juice. Add the coconut, marshmallows, orange rind, and orange sections and mix in well until evenly blended. Mix the yogurt, mayonnaise, and honey together until blended, then fold into the carrot-apple mixture. Stir together until everything is coated. Chill for at least 1 hour and serve cold on a bed of lettuce. Serves 8.

Lagniappe: This can be made completely in advance and stored in the refrigerator for up to 3 days. Of course, it is fresher if eaten the same day, but it does keep nicely. You can use this as a salad or a nice light dessert. Do not freeze.

Calories — 160; Carb — 20.5; Fat — 4.0; Chol — 0.7; Pro — 2.0; Fib — 1.4

SHRIMP SALAD

1 1/4 lb. boiled shrimp, peeled and deveined and chopped
1/4 cup green onions, chopped
1/4 cup green pepper, chopped
1/4 cup celery, chopped
1 clove garlic, minced
2 large hard-boiled eggs, chopped
1 cup light mayonnaise
1/4 cup stuffed olives, chopped
1 1/2 tbsp. fresh parsley, chopped
1 tbsp. fresh lime juice
1/4 tsp. Tabasco sauce
1/4 tsp. white pepper
1/2 tsp. black pepper
1 tsp. salt
1 tsp. sugar
1/4 cup sweet pickles, minced
1/4 tsp. tarragon
1 tsp. tarragon vinegar
1 tbsp. prepared horseradish
1/2 tsp. Creole mustard
1 medium head lettuce, shredded for salad bed
paprika for garnish

In a large mixing bowl, place all the ingredients except the lettuce and the paprika. Mix together well. Arrange the shredded lettuce on six plates or on shells and evenly place the shrimp mixture onto each plate. Sprinkle with the paprika and place lemon wedges on each side. Serve chilled. Serves 6 as a salad or main dish.

Lagniappe: You cannot freeze this dish, but you can make the salad, leave it in the mixing bowl, and cover it tightly until you are ready to serve. It will keep for up to 2 days in a cold refrigerator, but keep it tightly covered; plastic wrap works very well. When you are ready to serve, just put the lettuce on six serving plates and spoon the shrimp salad onto the lettuce. You can also serve this salad in avocado or tomato halves for a nice change.

Calories — 296; Carb — 11.1; Fat — 18.6; Chol — 234.2; Pro — 27.2; Fib — 0.9

FRESH CRAB SALAD

1 large hard-boiled egg,
   chopped
2 tbsp. celery, chopped
4 tbsp. light mayonnaise
1 tbsp. prepared
   horseradish
1 tsp. Dijon mustard
1 tbsp. fresh lemon juice
2 tbsp. green onions,
   chopped
1 tbsp. fresh parsley,
   chopped
1/4 tsp. Tabasco sauce

1/4 tsp. white pepper
1/2 tsp. black pepper
1 tsp. salt
1 tsp. sugar
1/4 cup sweet pickles,
   minced
1/4 tsp. sweet basil
1 lb. fresh lump crabmeat
3 large avocados
1 medium lemon
water
lettuce leaves for garnish
paprika for garnish

In a large mixing bowl, place all but the last six ingredients. Mix together well. Gently fold the crabmeat into the seasonings, taking care not to break apart the lumps. Cut the avocados in half and peel them. Scoop out some of the center. Cut the lemon in half and squeeze each half into a large bowl of water. Dip the peeled and cut avocados into the water and put them on a paper towel to dry.

Place the lettuce leaves on a serving plate or nice shell and place the avocado in the center. Fill the avocados with the crabmeat filling. Sprinkle a little paprika over each and serve chilled. Serves 6.

Lagniappe: You cannot freeze this dish, but you can make the whole salad, cover tightly with plastic wrap, and refrigerate until you are ready to serve. It looks nicer, though, if you wait to stuff the avocado halves. The salad will keep nicely for up to 2 days in the refrigerator; be sure to keep it very cold so the crabmeat won't spoil. To cut the calories even more, serve in a tomato half instead of the avocado.

Calories — 297; Carb — 13.8; Fat — 26.5; Chol — 121.9; Pro — 17.0; Fib — 2.3

TUNA AND MACARONI SALAD

2 cups cooked macaroni,
  rinsed in cold water and
  drained
1 can (12 1/2 oz.) tuna,
  water-packed, light and
  flaked
1 cup celery, chopped
1/4 cup green onions,
  chopped
1/4 cup stuffed olives,
  chopped
2 tbsp. green pepper,
  chopped
2 tbsp. sweet red pepper,
  chopped
2 tbsp. onion, chopped
1 tbsp. parsley, minced
1/2 tsp. salt
1/4 tsp. Tabasco sauce
1/4 tsp. white pepper
1 cup light mayonnaise
lettuce leaves for salad
  bed
paprika for garnish
lemon wedges for garnish

In a large mixing bowl, blend together well all but the last six ingredients. Mix together the Tabasco sauce, white pepper, and mayonnaise until smooth. Fold the mayonnaise into the macaroni-tuna mixture until it is well blended. Allow the salad to chill for 3 hours to let the flavors blend. For each serving, nicely arrange the lettuce leaves on a salad plate and place a large serving of salad on the leaves. Sprinkle with paprika and garnish with two lemon wedges. Serve cold. Serves 8.

Lagniappe: This can be made up to 48 hours in advance. It is an excellent alternative to a tuna sandwich. You are getting a complex carbohydrate instead of bread. This salad does not freeze and you should plan to use it all within 48 hours of making.

You can use the same recipe and substitute 2 cans of turkey meat to make **Turkey and Macaroni Salad** or substitute 2 cans of white chicken meat to make **Chicken and Macaroni Salad.** Use this salad anytime you need a quick salad.

TUNA: Calories—207; Carb—7.9; Fat—12.6; Chol—34.4; Pro—17.1; Fib—0.7

TURKEY: Calories — 223; Carb — 7.9; Fat — 13.7; Chol — 7.9; Pro — 6.5; Fib — 0.7

CHICKEN: Calories — 223; Carb — 7.9; Fat — 13.5; Chol — 6.1; Pro — 6.1; Fib — 0.7

CREAMY CUCUMBER AND TOMATO SALAD

1/4 cup green onions, minced
2 tbsp. fresh parsley, minced
1 tbsp. fresh lime juice
1/4 tsp. Tabasco sauce
2 tbsp. red wine vinegar
1/2 tsp. salt
1/4 tsp. white pepper

1/2 tsp. fresh ground black pepper
2 tsp. Dijon mustard
1 cup plain yogurt, low-fat
2 large firm red ripe tomatoes, cut into wedges
3 medium cucumbers, scored with a fork and sliced into circles

In a medium mixing bowl, mix all the ingredients together, except for the last two, until well combined. Blend in the tomatoes and cucumbers and mix to coat them well. Cover tightly to prevent any refrigerator odors from invading the dressing, and refrigerate for 2 hours. Serve chilled. Serves 6.

Lagniappe: This is an easy salad that will be somewhat unusual because of the green, red, and white colors. It can be made up to 1 day in advance, but it is better if served within 6 hours. Of course, you can't freeze this salad. You might also want to try this creamy yogurt dressing on just plain green salad; it has a nice, cool, light taste.

Calories — 56; Carb — 9.2; Fat — 0.9; Chol — 2.4; Pro — 3.0; Fib — 0.7

MEXICAN MIGHTY MOUSSE

2 tbsp. unflavored gelatin
3/4 cup cold water
2 medium avocados,
    peeled and pitted and
    diced
1/4 cup light mayonnaise
1/3 cup plain yogurt,
    low-fat
1 clove garlic, minced
1/4 cup picant sauce
1/4 tsp. Tabasco sauce
3/4 tsp. salt
1/4 cup lemon juice
1/4 cup lime juice

1/4 tsp. sweet basil
1/4 tsp. cumin powder
1/4 cup white onion,
    minced
1 medium fresh tomato,
    skinned and diced
2 tbsp. sweet green
    pepper, diced
2 tbsp. green onion,
    minced
1 tbsp. fresh parsley,
    minced
vegetable oil spray

Mix the gelatin with the cold water to soften it, then place over medium heat and heat until the gelatin is completely dissolved. Place all the remaining ingredients except for the last six into a food processor or blender and blend until smooth. Pour into the hot gelatin and mix in well. Add the remaining ingredients, except for the vegetable oil spray, and spoon the mixture into eight individual gelatin molds lightly greased with the vegetable spray. Chill until firmly set. Serve cold. Serves 8.

Lagniappe: This makes a nice salad or appetizer. It can be made up to 2 days in advance and unmolded when ready to serve. If you are going to leave in the refrigerator for any length of time, be sure to cover the bottom with plastic wrap to prevent odors from invading the gelatin. I like to serve it on a bed of lettuce.

Calories — 128; Carb — 8.6; Fat — 6.3; Chol — 0.6; Pro — 3.6; Fib — 1.2

PINEAPPLE-CELERY SALAD MOLD

2 tbsp. unflavored gelatin
3/4 cup cold water
2/3 cup celery, minced
2 cups unsweetened
  pineapple, crushed
1/4 cup sugar
1 1/2 tbsp. fresh lime juice

1 cup cottage cheese,
  low-fat, small curd
1 slice low-calorie American cheese, finely diced
4 packets Equal sweetener
2 cups Cool Whip
  non-dairy topping

In a medium saucepan, add the gelatin and water and stir to soften the gelatin. Add all but the last four ingredients and bring the gelatin-mixture to a low boil. Stir constantly and cook for 2 minutes. Remove from the heat, cool, and add the sweetener and two cheeses. Blend in well. Fold in the Cool Whip until smooth. Pour into eight individual, lightly greased gelatin molds. Chill until firmly set, at least 2 hours. Serve chilled. Serves 8.

Lagniappe: This dish can be made in advance and refrigerated for up to 3 days. Do not freeze. There are a number of different gelatin salads that can be made using this general recipe. Change the fruit and/or the celery. Gelatin molds look nice and tend to give the main dish more depth. Serve on a bed of lettuce leaves or shredded lettuce.

Calories — 170; Carb — 16.9; Fat — 4.7; Chol — 5.8; Pro — 6.4; Fib — 0.3

FRESH VEGETABLE SALAD

2 medium yellow squash
1 large zucchini
2 stalks celery, washed
and strings removed
1/2 lb. fresh green beans,
snapped and washed
1/2 lb. fresh asparagus,
trimmed
2 lb. small red new
potatoes
cold water to cover
1 tsp. salt

1/2 cup light mayonnaise
3 cloves garlic, minced
1 tsp. Creole mustard
1/4 tsp. Tabasco sauce
2 tbsp. fresh parsley,
minced
1/2 cup purple onion,
chopped
salt and black pepper to
taste
1 large boiled egg,
chopped

Place the yellow squash, zucchini, celery, green beans, and asparagus in a steamer and heat until the steam begins to rise. Let the vegetables steam for 1 minute, then turn the heat off, but leave them in the steamer.

In a large pot over medium-high heat, add the potatoes and cover them with the cold water. Add the salt and boil them until they are tender. Do not remove the red skin.

Slice the squash and zucchini into circles about 1/4-inch thick, break the beans in half, and chop the asparagus into about 1-inch-long pieces. Mix together well the light mayonnaise, garlic, Creole mustard, Tabasco sauce, and parsley. In a large mixing bowl, add the steamed vegetables, purple onion, boiled egg, and potatoes. Cover with the mayonnaise mixture, salt and pepper to taste, and toss until the salad is well mixed and coated with the mayonnaise dressing. Serve at once or refrigerate to serve cold. Serves 8.

Lagniappe: Do not freeze. This is an excellent vegetable salad that can substitute for potato salad at almost any function. You still have some of the potato salad taste but for fewer calories. It also provides a nice change from the ordinary.

You can make 2 main-dish salads in the following way. To make **Chicken Vegetable Salad,** just add 1 pound of diced cooked chicken breast to the recipe above. To make **Shrimp Vegetable Salad,** just add 1 1/4 pound of peeled and deveined boiled shrimp to the recipe above (talk about a real taste treat).

Calories – 171; Carb – 25.6; Fat – 6.9; Chol – 34.5; Pro – 6.1; Fib – 2.2

CRUNCHY APPLE SALAD

2 medium red apples
1 medium light green
   apple
1 tbsp. lemon juice
cold water for bath
1 cup celery, chopped
1/4 cup walnuts, chopped
1/4 cup light mayonnaise

1/4 cup plain yogurt,
   low-fat
1 tbsp. fresh lime juice
dash Tabasco sauce
1 tsp. sugar
1/2 tsp. red wine vinegar
1 tbsp. blue cheese,
   crumbled

Cut each apple in half and remove the cores. Thinly slice each apple lengthwise. Mix the lemon juice with enough water to cover all the apple slices. Put the apple slices into the lemon-water bath and let them soak for 1 minute. Remove and drain.

In a large mixing bowl, mix all the remaining ingredients except the cheese until well blended. Place the apple slices into the bowl with the celery-mayonnaise mixture and toss together until all the apple slices are coated. Refrigerate for at least 2 hours to allow the flavors to blend. Sprinkle with the blue cheese and serve chilled. Serves 6.

Lagniappe: You can make this dish up to 12 hours in advance; after that the apple slices will lose their crispness. Do not freeze. Serve on a bed of lettuce. This is an excellent sweet salad that is both tasty and light.

Calories – 128; Carb – 16.1; Fat – 6.0; Chol – 2.4; Pro – 2.4; Fib – 1.6

QUICK AND EASY
CHICKEN SALAD

3 cups cooked chicken,
  diced
1/2 cup light mayonnaise
1 tbsp. Dijon mustard
1 cup celery, finely diced
1/4 cup sweet bell pepper,
  diced
2 tbsp. pimento, diced
3 tbsp. green onions,
  minced

1/2 cup sweet pickle relish
3/4 tsp. onion powder
1/2 tsp. garlic powder
1/2 tsp. sweet basil
1/8 tsp. curry powder
1/4 tsp. Tabasco sauce
1 small purple onion,
  minced
1/2 tsp. salt
1 tsp. sugar

Combine ingredients together well. Chill in the refrigerator for at least 2 hours to allow blending of flavors. Serve chilled. Serves 6.

Lagniappe: To get the full flavor, this chicken salad should be made in advance. It can be refrigerated for up to 3 days before serving. It makes excellent sandwiches or you can stuff an avocado or tomato with it. I also like it just served on a bed of shredded lettuce. If you are going to make a sandwich, use the low-calorie bread (40 calories per slice) and your total sandwich will be under 200 calories per serving. A tomato stuffed with the chicken salad would have even fewer calories! Of course, if you want it really low, just serve on a lettuce bed.

Calories — 182; Carb — 12.2; Fat — 8.6; Chol — 36.5; Pro — 27.9; Fib — 0.5

GREEN ONION SALAD DRESSING

1 large egg, lightly beaten
1 tbsp. lemon juice
1/4 cup red wine vinegar
1/2 tsp. dry hot mustard
1/2 tsp. sugar
1/2 tsp. honey
1/2 tsp. salt
1/4 cup cold water

1 cup green onions,
    chopped
1 cup fresh parsley,
    minced
1/4 tsp. Tabasco sauce
1/2 cup pure vegetable
    salad oil, no saturated
    fats

In a food processor or blender, add the first seven ingredients and mix at high speed for 3 minutes. The egg should be quite frothy. While the processor is running, drizzle in the water. Stop and add the green onions. Return to high speed for 2 minutes or until the onions have been completely processed. Add the parsley, return to high speed, and blend until the parsley is completely processed and blended into the liquid. Add the Tabasco and turn the processor on; drizzle in the vegetable oil slowly until it is beaten into the dressing. Serve either at once or chilled. Makes about 1 1/2 cups.

Lagniappe: You can make this dressing up to 2 days in advance. It will start to separate, but just shake it vigorously and it should blend back together. It makes a nice salad dressing that is lower in calories than most made with 100 percent oil. It is nice over any green salad.

PER TABLESPOON: Calories—49; Carb—1.6; Fat—1.6; Chol—11.5; Pro—0.4; Fib—0.2

RUSSIAN DRESSING

1 cup light mayonnaise
1/4 cup fresh lemon juice
1/4 cup skim milk
1/4 cup stuffed olives,
    chopped
1/8 cup chili sauce
2 tbsp. green onions,
    minced

2 tbsp. onions, minced
2 tbsp. green pepper,
    minced
2 tbsp. prepared
    horseradish
1 tbsp. red wine vinegar
1/4 tsp. Tabasco sauce
1/2 tsp. salt

In a large mixing bowl, combine all ingredients with either a wire whisk or an electric blender (you can just add it all to a food processor and blend). Whip together until well blended. Makes about 2 cups.

Lagniappe: You can make this dressing well in advance. In fact, it keeps very well in the refrigerator for up to a week. This Russian dressing will almost taste as rich as the real thing, with fewer calories.

PER TABLESPOON: Calories — 31; Carb — 1.0; Fat — 2.9; Chol — Trace; Pro — 0.3; Fib — 0.1

POPPY SEED DRESSING

1 small clove garlic, minced	1/4 tsp. Tabasco sauce
1 tbsp. onion, chopped	1 tbsp. sugar
2 tbsp. white vinegar	2 tbsp. honey
1/2 tsp. dry mustard	2 tbsp. water
1 tsp. fresh lemon juice	4 tbsp. corn vegetable oil
	1 tbsp. poppy seeds

In a food processor or blender, add the garlic and onion. Blend at high speed for 1 minute. Add the vinegar, dry mustard, lemon juice, and Tabasco sauce and blend at high speed 1 more minute. Add the sugar, honey, and water and blend until the sugar is dissolved. Let the motor run and drizzle the oil through the top slowly to allow it to whip in well. When all the oil is added, drop the poppy seeds through the opening and let them mix in well. Pour into a container that has a lid and store in the refrigerator. This dressing is excellent over fruit or over a green salad. Makes about 1 cup.

Lagniappe: This dressing can be made in advance and stored in the refrigerator for up to 2 weeks. It may begin to separate, but just shake it vigorously and it will blend again. You can double this recipe if necessary. This dressing really brings out the sweetness of melons or any tart fruit.

PER TABLESPOON: Calories—45; Carb—3.2; Fat—3.5; Chol—Trace; Pro—0.2; Fib—Trace

SHERRY-YOGURT SALAD DRESSING

1/2 cup cream sherry
1 cup yogurt
1 1/2 cups light mayon-
   naise
1 tsp. rosemary, finely
   crushed

1/4 tsp. Tabasco sauce
1 tsp. tarragon, finely
   crushed
1 tsp. garlic powder
1 tsp. onion powder
2 drops red food coloring

In a large mixing bowl, add all ingredients and blend well with a wire whisk. Refrigerate for at least 2 hours before using. Works well over any salad greens. Makes about 2 1/2 cups.

Lagniappe: You can make this dressing in advance and store up to 1 week in the refrigerator. Do not freeze. This is a light dressing, yet very tasty. For variety you can change the herbs. Basil is a nice addition as well as chives, chervil, or dill. Use the combinations you like.

PER TABLESPOON: Calories — 39; Carb — 1.4; Fat — 3.1; Chol — 0.4; Pro — 0.5; Fib — Trace

Sauces

I bet you never expected to find a sauce section in a low-calorie cookbook. Well, surprise, surprise! Sauces are important for giving food that zest and taste appeal that make a great meal even more enjoyable.

Some of the sauces you will find here are just light versions of sauces that you might already know. Others are my own creations. With both kinds of sauces you will lift your low-calorie dishes from the bland to the exciting. A little care and quality will go a long way toward making your meals more pleasurable.

Sauces should not be left out just because you are watching your calories. Use the sauces within to help you add elegance to your dishes and a smile to the faces of your diners.

LIGHT BUTTER SAU

1 packet (1/2 oz.) Butter
  Buds
1/4 cup very hot water
3 tbsp. chicken stock or
  chicken broth

1/2 tsp.
  tersh
1/8 tsp
1/4 tsp

Mix the packet of Butter Buds with the hot water. Stir un..
solved. Mix in other ingredients and blend well. Use as a butter sauce
over vegetables, seafood, or meats. Makes about 1/2 cup.

Lagniappe: You can mix this sauce in advance and refrigerate until you
    are ready to use. Just warm over low heat. You'll love the taste of
    "real" butter and for almost no calories.

*PER TABLESPOON: Calories — 7; Carb — 3.0; Fat — Trace; Chol —
0.1; Pro — 0.4; Fib — 0.0*

SAUCE DIJON

1 cup Hollandaise Light
  (see index for recipe)
3 tbsp. Dijon mustard

1 tbsp. dry vermouth
1/8 tsp. ground nutmeg

Make a recipe of Hollandaise Light. Mix together well the Dijon mustard and vermouth. After the hollandaise is complete, use the wire
whisk to whip in the Dijon-vermouth mixture and the nutmeg and
parsley. Use over chicken or seafood. Makes about 1 1/4 cups.

Lagniappe: This sauce must be made just before you are ready to use.
    It will not store in the refrigerator or the freezer. You can let it stand
    at room temperature for up to 1 hour before using. This is an excel-
    lent sauce for baked or poached seafood.

*PER TABLESPOON: Calories — 40; Carb — 0.4; Fat — 1.9; Chol —
27.4; Pro — 0.8; Fib — Trace*

LIGHT MORNAY SAUCE

sp. diet margarine
bsp. flour
/4 cup skim milk, warm
1/4 cup chicken stock or
  chicken broth

1/8 tsp. Tabasco sauce
1/8 tsp. white pepper
1/2 tsp. salt
1/4 cup Swiss cheese,
  grated

In a saucepan over medium heat, melt the margarine. Add the flour and, using a wire whisk, blend into the margarine. Cook for 3 minutes over medium heat, stirring constantly. Remove from the heat and add the skim milk, chicken stock, and Tabasco. Blend in well and return to the heat; cook while whisking until the sauce thickens and is smooth. Add the remaining ingredients and blend in well. Whisk until the cheese melts. Remove and keep warm. Serve over meats, vegetables, and fish. Makes about 1 cup.

Lagniappe: The taste of this sauce is quite close to the "real" Mornay and I think you will find it a suitable substitute. This sauce can be refrigerated for later use, but do not freeze. Just heat it over low heat, while stirring with a whisk.

If you are not worried about calories or cholesterol, you can use butter instead of the diet margarine and whole milk instead of the skim.

PER TABLESPOON: Calories — 51; Carb — 1.4; Fat — 1.8; Chol — 3.5; Pro — 1.6; Fib — Trace

MADE WITH BUTTER AND WHOLE MILK: Calories — 75; Carb — 1.4; Fat — 2.2; Chol — 9.1; Pro — 1.6; Fib — Trace

SEAFOOD DIPPING SAUCE

1 cup reduced calorie
  catsup
1 cup light mayonnaise
1 tbsp. Tabasco sauce

2 tbsp. fresh lemon juice
1 tbsp. Worcestershire
  sauce
1 tsp. red wine vinegar

Mix all of the ingredients together and let stand for 1 hour to blend the flavors fully. You can use this as a dipping sauce for boiled or broiled seafood or you can lightly sauce the seafood before serving. Makes about 2 1/4 cups.

Lagniappe: This sauce can be made up to 48 hours in advance. Because it is so spicy, it goes a long way. This is excellent with any seafood.

PER TABLESPOON: Calories — 28; Carb — 1.5; Fat — 2.0; Chol — Trace; Pro — 0.3; Fib — Trace

GREEN PEPPERCORN SAUCE

1 tbsp. diet margarine
1 1/2 tsp. shallots, minced
1/2 clove garlic, minced
4 tbsp. green peppercorns,
  whole, drained from
  liquid (not dried)
2 tsp. all-purpose flour
1/4 cup dry white wine
1/4 cup skim milk

1/2 cup chicken stock or
  chicken broth
1/4 tsp. Tabasco sauce
6 tsp. Butter Buds
1 tsp. fresh parsley,
  minced
1/4 tsp. sweet basil
1/8 tsp. dried dill weed or
  1 sprig fresh dill

In a small saucepan over medium heat, melt the margarine. Add the shallots and garlic and sauté for 2 minutes. Add the green peppercorns and continue to sauté for 3 more minutes. Add the flour and cook for 2 minutes, stirring constantly. Add the wine and blend in, then add the milk and chicken stock. Stir until well mixed. Add the remaining ingredients and cook, stirring, for 3 more minutes or until the sauce thickens. Serve hot over meats or seafood. Makes about 1 cup.

Lagniappe: This sauce can be made in advance and refrigerated; it will not freeze well. To use, just reheat while stirring and serve. You can change the spices in this sauce to create different tastes.

PER TABLESPOON: Calories — 37; Carb — 1.8; Fat — 0.5; Chol — 0.1; Pro — 0.5; Fib — 0.1

HOLLANDAISE LIGHT

6 tsp. Butter Buds
1/8 cup hot water
2 large eggs
1 tbsp. fresh lemon juice
1/2 tsp. dry hot mustard

1/4 tsp. white pepper
1/4 tsp. salt
1/8 tsp. Tabasco sauce
1/2 stick diet margarine,
  melted

Dissolve the Butter Buds in the hot water, and set aside. In a large metal mixing bowl, beat the eggs with a wire whisk for 2 minutes. Add the Butter Buds liquid that you set aside and all the remaining ingredients except for the margarine. Add to the eggs, beating until well blended.

Boil a little water in a saucepan that is small enough for the bottom of the metal bowl to rest on top of. When the water is boiling, reduce the heat to a simmer that is high enough to let a little steam rise from the water. Place the metal bowl on top of the saucepan and constantly whisk the egg mixture (if you stop you get scrambled eggs). The mixture will thicken to the consistency of unset pudding. Slowly start adding the margarine until it is all added. Be sure to continue whisking as the margarine is added. If the bowl gets too hot to touch, it is too hot for the egg mixture, so lift it off until the bowl cools somewhat. The sauce is ready when the margarine is all beaten in. Let stand at room temperature for at least 5 minutes. Makes about 1 cup.

Lagniappe: Make this sauce as you need it. It will not keep well in the refrigerator. You can keep it at room temperature for 30 or so minutes before serving. This is about as close as I could get to "real" hollandaise taste for so few calories. Regular hollandaise has about 66 calories per tablespoon, so this is a significant improvement.

PER TABLESPOON: Calories — 26; Carb — 0.4; Fat — 2.2; Chol — 34.3; Pro — 0.8; Fib — Trace

CAPER SAUCE

1 packet (1/2 oz.) Butter
   Buds
1/3 cup hot water
2 large brown eggs, beaten
2 tbsp. fresh lemon juice
1/8 tsp. nutmeg
1/4 tsp. salt
1/4 tsp. cayenne pepper
1 tbsp. celery, minced

4 tbsp. capers,
   well-drained
1 tsp. fresh parsley,
   minced
1/4 tsp. Tabasco sauce
2 tbsp. diet margarine,
   softened and cut into
   pieces

Mix the Butter Buds with the hot water until dissolved. Add the Butter Buds liquid to the eggs. Use a wire whisk and blend well. Add the lemon juice, nutmeg, salt, and cayenne pepper. Pour the mixture into the top of a double boiler that has water in the bottom and place over low heat. Stir constantly with the whisk until the sauce begins to thicken. Add the capers, celery, parsley, and Tabasco sauce and continue cooking until the sauce is thick enough to coat the back of a spoon. Add the softened margarine and whisk it slowly into the sauce. Serve over chicken, meat, or seafood. Makes about 1 cup.

Lagniappe: This sauce needs to be made just before you are ready to serve. It will not take freezing or refrigeration. You can let it sit at room temperature for 30 minutes to an hour.

PER TABLESPOON: Calories—25; Carb—0.6; Fat—1.5; Chol—34.3; Pro—0.8; Fib—Trace

TARTAR SAUCE

1 cup light mayonnaise
1 tbsp. Dijon mustard
1 small onion, minced
1 clove garlic, minced
1/2 cup dill pickle, minced
1 tbsp. sweet pickle relish
2 tbsp. stuffed olives,
  chopped

2 tbsp. pimentos, diced
1/4 tsp. Tabasco sauce
1/2 tsp. fresh lime juice
1 tsp. fresh parsley,
  minced
1 tsp. dry hot mustard
1/2 tsp. cream of tartar

Mix together all ingredients well, then chill until ready to serve. Serve with seafood. Makes about 2 cups.

Lagniappe: You can store this sauce in the refrigerator for 3 to 4 days. Keep it tightly covered and cold. Do not freeze. This is an easy and excellent tartar sauce to serve with any baked, broiled, or fried seafood.

PER TABLESPOON: Calories—29; Carb—1.2; Fat—2.7; Chol— Trace; Pro—0.3; Fib—0.1

Seafood

This is the fun section. Seafoods offer such a variety of choices to the cook. Try them all! They are generally low in calories and fat. Stick with fresh fish whenever possible. One general way to determine if the fish is fresh is by smell. Seafood smells like seafood, but it shouldn't make you pull away; if it does, then by all means do! The longer it sits the more the odor will grow.

When fresh fish is not available, properly frozen fish is satisfactory. The best way to insure proper freezing is to do it yourself. Placing seafood in a container full of water and then freezing is a good method. Supermarkets now offer a wider and wider variety of fresh seafood, some even so fresh that they are alive and swimming when you purchase them.

There is a great deal of new research with fish oil. Keep up with the current facts. It appears the cholesterol in oily fish may by beneficial. If this is fully substantiated, seafood will be regarded as an even greater benefit to our diets.

You will find these recipes are easy to use and superior in taste. Seafood lends itself well to creating memorable dishes. The main caution is, "please don't overcook." Seafood is mainly water. When you overcook, all you are doing is removing the water. What you are left with is a tasteless mass that is lacking in texture and appearance. Most seafood cooks quite quickly. Follow the directions and do not add a few minutes "just for good measure." Your good intentions will destroy the dish. If cooked properly, there is nothing better than seafood.

SPICY BOILED BASS MORNAY

1/2 gal. water
2 cloves garlic, crushed
1/2 bunch green onions,
  cut into thirds
4 sprigs parsley
2 stalks celery, cut into
  thirds
2 large bay leaves
1 tbsp. fresh basil or 1 tsp.
  dried
5 whole cloves
5 whole allspice, crushed
10 whole black
  peppercorns

1 whole lemon, cut into
  circles
1 small red pepper
2 tsp. salt
1 tsp. thyme
1/2 tsp. tarragon
8 3-oz. bass fillets
1 cup Light Mornay Sauce
  (see index for recipe)
lemon wedges for garnish
fresh sprigs of parsley for
  garnish
paprika for garnish

In a large stockpot over high heat, bring the water to a boil. Add all the ingredients up to the bass fillets, reduce the heat to a low rolling boil, and boil for 10 minutes to allow the spices to blend into the water. Drop in the bass fillets and boil in the low-rolling water for 10 minutes, then carefully remove with a slotted spoon. Drain quickly and arrange 2 bass fillets on each of four heated serving plates. Spoon 1 tablespoon of Mornay sauce over each bass fillet and garnish with lemon wedges and parsley sprigs. Sprinkle with paprika and serve. Serves 4.

Lagniappe: You can make your Mornay sauce in advance, but do not cook the bass in advance. This is an easy recipe and quite tasty. The only thing that has to be watched is that the water not be at a hard boil, which would tear the fish. Take particular care when removing the fish, so you don't break it apart. I would suggest serving broccoli, asparagus, or greens with this dish to add color. You are not limited to bass; you can use your favorite fish fillets as a substitute.

Calories—321; Carb—11.3; Fat—5.4; Chol—123.5; Pro—34.0; Fib—1.3

DEVILED CRABS

3 cups French bread, torn into small pieces
1/2 cup skim milk
1 lb. lump crabmeat, fresh
2 large brown eggs, beaten
1/2 cup light mayonnaise
1 tbsp. Dijon mustard
1/2 tsp. Tabasco sauce
1 tsp. salt
1/4 tsp. white pepper
1/4 tsp. cayenne pepper
1 tsp. Worcestershire sauce
1 1/2 tbsp. fresh lemon juice
1 tbsp. butter, unsalted
1 tbsp. diet margarine
1/2 cup onions, minced
1/4 cup green onions, minced
1/4 cup bell pepper, minced
1/4 cup celery, minced
2 tbsp. pimento, diced
2 tbsp. fresh parsley, minced

Preheat the oven to 350 degrees. Pour the French bread into a mixing bowl and pour the skim milk over it. Press the bread into the milk. Let stand for 2 minutes. Using your hands, squeeze the milk out of the bread and put the squeezed bread into a large mixing bowl. Add the crabmeat, eggs, mayonnaise, mustard, salt, peppers, Worcestershire sauce, and lemon juice. Mix together well, then cover tightly with plastic wrap and refrigerate.

In a saucepan over medium heat, melt the butter and margarine. When melted, sauté the onions, bell pepper, and celery for 4 minutes, then set aside to cool. Remove the crabmeat mixture from the refrigerator and add the cooled sautéed vegetables, liquid and all, to the bowl. Add the green onions, pimento, and parsley. Mix together until completely blended. Divide the mixture into six ceramic shells or put into twelve of the aluminum foil crab shells or, if you want to bother cleaning real crab shells very carefully, you can use twelve real shells. Dust with paprika and bake for 30 minutes at 350 degrees. Serve hot. Serves 6.

Lagniappe: This is an excellent make-ahead dish. You can make to the stuffing point and cover and refrigerate until you are ready to use. The stuffed crabs will keep for up to 48 hours in the refrigerator. You can also tightly wrap each shell and freeze. It keeps well for up to 1 month frozen. When you are ready to use, just thaw in the refrigerator and bake as above. This is fine eating! The deviled crabs can also be breaded with flour or breadcrumbs and deep-fried, but you will be adding significantly to the calorie count.

Calories — 288; Carb — 16.9; Fat — 14.3; Chol — 173.4; Pro — 17.5; Fib — 0.5

GRILLED FRESH
CATFISH FILLETS

2 tbsp. peanut oil
2 tbsp. diet margarine,
  melted
2 tbsp. soy sauce
1 tsp. white
  Worcestershire sauce
1 tsp. tarragon vinegar
3 tsp. Butter Buds

1 tsp. fresh ground ginger
1/4 tsp. Tabasco sauce
1/4 tsp. white pepper
1/2 tsp. salt
6 fillets catfish, about
  6 oz. each and 1-inch
  thick

Mix together all the ingredients but the fillets in a small sauté pan and simmer over low heat for 3 minutes, then remove from the heat and allow the marinade to cool completely. Lay the fish down in a shallow pan and pour the mixture over the fish. Cover and refrigerate for 2 hours.

Get your grill coals very hot and grill the fish about 3 minutes per side. Baste often with the marinade during the grilling. Serve at once. Serves 6.

Lagniappe: There is almost nothing to this recipe but the taste! You can do the marinade well in advance and marinate the fish for up to 36 hours before grilling. If you do choose to marinate for any length of time, just turn the fish every 4 to 6 hours and keep covered. This is a great way to have an outdoor grill when you are trying to stay away from meat.

Calories — 243; Carb — 1.4; Fat — 11.8; Chol — 42.9; Pro — 30.8; Fib — Trace

SIMMERING CATFISH

1 tbsp. Worcestershire
  sauce
2 tbsp. dry vermouth
1 tbsp. soy sauce
1/4 tbsp. Tabasco sauce
1 tbsp. cornstarch
1 lb. catfish fillets, cut into
  strips crosswise
1 cup carrots, julienned
1 cup celery, julienned

1 cup cauliflower florets
1 cup sweet red bell pep-
  per, julienned
water for steamer
2 tbsp. peanut oil
2 cloves garlic, minced
1 tsp. shallots, minced
1 tsp. sugar
1/4 tsp. sweet basil
1/2 tsp. dry hot mustard

In a large mixing bowl, combine the Worcestershire sauce, vermouth, soy sauce, Tabasco, and cornstarch and blend together until cornstarch is dissolved. Add the catfish strips to the bowl and coat them well. Let the fish marinate in the liquid for 15 minutes. Add the carrots, celery, cauliflower, and red pepper to a steamer and place a little water in the bottom. Bring to a full boil and when the steam begins to rise strongly, time 2 minutes. Remove from the fire and let the vegetables stand in the steamer for 5 minutes. Remove, drain, and set aside for later use.

When the catfish has finished marinating, heat a large skillet over medium-high heat until the pan is hot. Add the peanut oil and wait for it to smoke. Add the fish, garlic, and shallots, taking care not to get splashed with the oil. Sauté quickly until the fish is lightly brown, but white inside, about 3 to 5 minutes. The fish will puff slightly. Add the vegetables, the remaining marinade, and the remaining ingredients and mix together well. Serve at once. Serves 4.

Lagniappe: This dish cannot be refrigerated or frozen. You can do all the preparations in advance, like steaming the vegetables and marinating the catfish, so all that will be left is the quick cooking process. You can let the fish stay in the marinade overnight. Serve this dish over rice, if you like, or over cooked noodles or spaghetti. It is also okay to use different fish fillets if you desire.

Calories — 229; Carb — 10.5; Fat — 9.3; Chol — 28.6; Pro — 22.3; Fib — 1.0

SCALLOPS YOLANDE

1 1/2 lb. fresh bay scallops
vegetable oil spray
2 tbsp. diet margarine
2 cloves garlic, minced
1 tsp. shallots, minced
1/2 cup sweet red
   bell pepper, julienned
1/2 tsp. oregano
1 1/4 tsp. salt
1/2 tsp. red pepper

1/4 tsp. white pepper
1/8 tsp. rosemary,
   crumbled
1/8 tsp. sweet basil
1 medium bay leaf
1/3 cup extra dry sherry
2 tbsp. lemon juice
1/4 cup fresh parsley,
   chopped
3 cups cooked white rice

Look over the scallops to make sure there are no hard muscles left. If you find any, cut them out. Spray a large, heavy nonstick skillet with the vegetable oil spray and place over medium-high heat. When the skillet is hot, add the margarine. When it begins to smoke, add the scallops, garlic, and shallots. Sauté, stirring constantly for 3 minutes. Add the sweet red bell pepper and sauté for 30 seconds. Sprinkle in the seasonings and mix in well. Pour in the sherry and lemon juice and reduce the heat to simmer. Simmer for 3 more minutes or until the scallops are puffy and a nice white color. Add the parsley, mix together, then serve at once over 1/2 cup of cooked white rice per serving. Serves 6.

Lagniappe: This is the perfect quick meal. If you get a call that you are going to have six for dinner and don't know what to serve, now you know. It is easy and so delicious. Scallops are a little out of the ordinary so it makes them special. You can add the rice right to the dish if you like and serve as a one-dish meal. Either way, the dish is dynamite!

Calories — 232; Carb — 28.6; Fat — 2.7; Chol — 40.0; Pro — 19.9; Fib — 0.3

CRABMEAT ASPARAGUS

2 tbsp. diet margarine
2 tbsp. all-purpose flour
1 cup chicken stock or
　chicken broth
2 tbsp. dry white wine
1/4 tsp. Tabasco sauce
1/4 tsp. sweet basil
1/4 tsp. white pepper
1/2 tsp. salt
1/2 lb. fresh asparagus,
　trimmed and steamed
　until cooked

1/4 tsp. dry hot mustard
1 lb. fresh lump crabmeat
1/4 cup green onions,
　chopped
1/4 cup fresh parsley,
　minced
3 slices low-calorie Swiss
　cheese, minced
3 large eggs, whites only
2 tbsp. light mayonnaise
1/4 tsp. paprika

Preheat the oven to 350 degrees. In a saucepan over medium heat, melt the margarine, then blend in the flour until it is well mixed. Cook over medium heat for 2 minutes; remove from the heat and add the chicken stock and white wine. Blend well with a wire whisk, then return to the heat and cook, stirring constantly, until the sauce thickens. Add the Tabasco sauce, basil, white pepper, salt, and dry hot mustard. Whisk until blended. Cover the bottom of a shallow 2 quart casserole with just enough sauce to cover. Spread one-half of the asparagus over the sauce. Mix together the crabmeat, green onions, and parsley, taking care not to tear the lumps of crab. Gently spread one-half of the crab mixture over the asparagus and spoon just enough of the sauce to cover the crabmeat evenly. Add the remaining asparagus to cover the crab-meat, then cover it with the remaining crabmeat. Pour the remaining sauce over the top of the casserole. Sprinkle with the Swiss cheese and bake at 350 degrees for 20 minutes.

While the casserole is baking, beat the egg whites until they form stiff peaks. Whip in the light mayonnaise and paprika. Remove the cas-serole from the oven when cooked; turn the oven to broil. Spread the meringue over the top of the dish to cover lightly all the casserole. Place in the oven about 8 to 10 inches from the heat and let the meringue brown. Serve at once.

Lagniappe: This is real company dining, yet reasonable in calorie count. You can make the dish up to the point of baking and refrigerate until ready to serve. This actually helps to let the flavors blend. It will keep for up to 48 hours, but I would suggest waiting only about 8, because the sauce can begin to water. When you are ready to serve, just bake, make the meringue, and continue as above. This dish also really looks nice served in individual ramekins. You can add richness by using real butter in place of the diet margarine, regular Swiss cheese in place of the low-calorie variety, and regular mayonnaise in place of the light mayonnaise.

LOW-CALORIE VERSION: Calories—175; Carb—5.7; Fat—6.7; Chol—84.4; Pro—22.0; Fib—0.6

WITH REGULAR INGREDIENTS: Calories—243; Carb—6.4; Fat—6.4; Chol—102.2; Pro—22.3; Fib—0.6

CHILI FROM THE SEA

1 cup peanut oil
1/2 lb. catfish fillets, diced
1/2 lb. red snapper fillets, diced
1/2 lb. redfish fillets, diced
1/2 lb. fresh bay scallops
1/2 lb. small shrimp, peeled and deveined
2 large onions, chopped
3 cloves garlic, minced
1 medium bell pepper, chopped
1/2 cup celery, chopped
1 can (15 oz.) stewed tomatoes
1 can (10 oz.) Rotel stewed tomatoes
1/4 cup chili powder
2 tbsp. paprika

1 tbsp. cumin powder
1 tsp. garlic powder
1 tsp. onion powder
1/2 tsp. oregano
1/2 tsp. sweet basil
1/2 tsp. red pepper
1/2 tsp. black pepper
1 1/2 tsp. salt
1/2 tsp. Tabasco sauce
2 tbsp. Worcestershire sauce
1 can (15 oz.) tomato sauce
1 cup tomato juice
1 cup oysters, whole
1/2 lb. lump crabmeat
1 cup green onions, minced

Heat the oil in a large saucepan over medium-high heat. When the oil is hot, add the fish, scallops, and shrimp. Cook for 3 minutes, stirring often. Add the onions and garlic and cook for 2 more minutes. Then add the bell pepper and celery and sauté for 2 more minutes. Add both cans stewed tomatoes, but take care not to add the liquid at this time. Sauté for 2 more minutes. Add the spices, Tabasco sauce, and Worcestershire sauce and blend in well. Reduce the heat to a simmer, and add the liquid from the stewed tomatoes, tomato sauce, and tomato juice; mix in well, then cover and let simmer for 30 minutes over low heat. Five minutes before you are ready to serve, add the oysters, crabmeat, and green onions and mix in well. Continue to let the seafood chili simmer for the 5 minutes. Serve hot. Serves 12.

Lagniappe: You can make this chili in advance and refrigerate or freeze. It actually improves with age. It is a hearty stock and very rich. Feel free to substitute whatever type of fish you may have on hand for those listed. Just keep the proportions the same. This is an easy dish that is particularly good for cold nights.

Calories—363; Carb—12.2; Fat—20.2; Chol—276.1; Pro—34.3; Fib—1.7

SHRIMP CAKES

1 lb. boiled shrimp, peeled and deveined
2 tbsp. fresh parsley, minced
1/4 cup green onions, minced
1/4 tsp. Tabasco sauce
1 tbsp. diet margarine, softened

1 tbsp. red wine vinegar
2 tsp. Worcestershire sauce
1/2 tsp. sweet basil
1/8 tsp. nutmeg
1/2 cup light mayonnaise
seasoned bread crumbs
2 tbsp. peanut oil

Either mince the shrimp with a food processor or run the shrimp through a meat grinder. In a large mixing bowl, add all the ingredients except the bread crumbs and the peanut oil. Mix together well. Form into cakes about the size of hamburger patties. You should be able to make about 6 nice-sized cakes or 12 small cakes. Roll the cakes in the bread crumbs and set them in a pan that has a tight cover. Refrigerate for 2 hours.

When ready to cook, add the peanut oil to a large skillet over medium-high heat and get the oil hot. Then add each of the cakes and dry on each side until golden brown. Take care when turning the cakes so that they do not break apart. Serve hot. Serves 6.

Lagniappe: These cakes can be made in advance and either refrigerated (for up to 48 hours) or frozen for later use. Just thaw in the refrigerator and continue with the cooking process. You can lower the calorie count by 40 per serving by baking the cakes in the oven at 350 degrees on a cookie sheet that has been sprayed with Pam for about 25 minutes. Or you can deep-fry them and add about 100 calories per serving. For deep-frying, I suggest smaller cakes and for baking, the larger ones.

You can make **Crab Cakes** using the same recipe as above by substituting 1 pound of lump crabmeat for the shrimp. You would not need to grind the crabmeat to make this dish.

SHRIMP: Calories — 205; Carb — 5.6; Fat — 12.8; Chol — 119.6; Pro — 15.4; Fib — 0.2

CRAB: Calories — 202; Carb — 4.9; Fat — 13.7; Chol — 81.5; Pro — 14.3; Fib — 0.2

OYSTER CASSEROLE NOELIE

1 large eggplant, peeled
water to cover
2 tsp. salt
vegetable oil spray, butter
  flavor
1/4 cup hot water
1 packet (1/2 oz.) Butter
  Buds
2 large eggs, beaten
1/2 cup evaporated skim
  milk
1/2 cup skim milk
1/2 cup green onions,
  chopped

3 cups fresh oysters with
  their juice
1/4 tsp. Tabasco sauce
1/2 tsp. salt
1/2 tsp. black pepper
1/2 tsp. garlic powder
1 tsp. onion powder
1/4 tsp. sweet basil
1/3 cup fresh bread
  crumbs made from light
  bread
1 tsp. fresh parsley
paprika for garnish

Preheat the oven to 350 degrees. Place the eggplant whole into the water, with the 2 teaspoons of salt, and bring to a boil. Boil for 3 minutes, then let the eggplant sit in the water for 5 more minutes. Remove and drain. When it is cool, chop it up into small pieces. Spray the bottom of a 2-quart shallow baking dish with the vegetable oil spray, and set aside for later use.

Mix together the 1/4 cup of hot water and the Butter Buds and stir until dissolved. Mix together the eggplant, eggs, evaporated skim milk, skim milk, Butter Buds mixture, and green onions in a large mixing bowl. In a medium saucepan over medium heat, add the oysters and their liquid. Bring to a boil and cook until they puff up and the edges curl. (Do not overcook; you will make them tough and disappear, since they are mainly water). Remove from the heat and drain the oysters on paper towels. Add the oysters to the eggplant mixture and blend in. Season with the Tabasco sauce, salt, pepper, garlic powder, onion powder, and sweet basil; mix together well. Pour into the oiled serving dish and sprinkle the bread crumbs on top. Lightly spray with the vegetable oil spray and bake for 20 minutes at 350 degrees. Open the oven and sprinkle with fresh parsley and paprika. Bake for 15 more minutes. Serve hot. Serves 6.

Lagniappe: This dish can be made up to the baking point and refrigerated for up to 24 hours, or it can be baked and frozen for later use. I like to make one extra, when I am making one to eat that day. Cover tightly with plastic wrap and freeze. When you are ready to serve, just thaw in the refrigerator and bake at 300 degrees until hot, about 10 minutes. If you refrigerated, just follow the recipe from where you left off. Oysters do different things for different people. Some people can't even try them. If you haven't tried a baked oyster, don't judge all oyster dishes by their uncooked brethren! When baked they are divine.

Calories—175; Carb—12.1; Fat—4.6; Chol—320.8; Pro—15.5; Fib—1.0

POACHED SALMON WITH GREEN PEPPERCORN SAUCE

**4 steaks salmon,
about 5 oz. each
1 cup water
1 cup dry white wine**

**1/2 tsp. salt
1 cup Green Peppercorn
Sauce (see index
for recipe)**

Wash the steaks in cold water and pat dry with a paper towel. In a medium skillet that has a cover, bring the water and wine to a boil. When boiling, add the salt and the salmon, then reduce the heat to a simmer. Cover, and cook for 5 minutes. Uncover and turn the steaks carefully to the other side. Cover again and cook for 5 more minutes. Remove the steaks from the water and let them drain. Place each on a warm plate and serve with 2 tablespoons of the Green Peppercorn Sauce per steak. Serve at once. Serves 4.

Lagniappe: You cannot poach fish until you are ready to serve. Cooking time is only 10 minutes for the fish and you can make the sauce in advance, so this dish is easy to prepare.

WITH 2 TABLESPOONS OF SAUCE: Calories—430; Carb—5.6; Fat—20.1; Chol—50.2; Pro—33.3; Fib—Trace

AUNT NET'S OYSTERS ELEGANTE

2 dozen large oysters
3 cloves garlic, minced
1 tsp. salt
1/2 tsp. white pepper
1/2 tsp. red pepper
1/4 tsp. sweet basil
2 tbsp. Worcestershire sauce
1 bunch green onions, minced
1/2 cup fresh parsley, minced

5 slices light whole wheat bread (40 calories per slice)
1/4 cup diet margarine
1/2 cup bell pepper, diced
1/4 cup celery, minced
2 tbsp. fresh lemon juice
2 tbsp. extra dry vermouth
1/2 tsp. dry hot mustard
2 1/2 tsp. Butter Buds
1/4 tsp. Tabasco sauce

Remove the oysters from their liquid and pat them dry with paper towels. Arrange them on the bottom of a 2-quart shallow baking dish. Season with the garlic, salt, white pepper, red pepper, and sweet basil. Pour the Worcestershire sauce around the oysters and sprinkle the green onions and parsley on top of them.

Take the bread and cut it into slices 1/2-inch wide. Then cut again 1/2-inch wide. This will give you bread squares about 1/2-inch on all sides. Sprinkle this bread on top of the onions and parsley.

In a small sauté pan, melt the margarine over medium heat, then sauté the bell pepper and celery for 5 minutes. Add the remaining ingredients to the sauté and blend together well. Pour this sauté over the bread as evenly as possible. Bake at 400 degrees for about 12 minutes or until the bread is brown and the oysters begin to curl around the edges. Serve hot. Serves 4.

Lagniappe: This is really a nice oyster dish, and very easy. Don't let the list of ingredients make you think that it's hard. I like to serve this in individual serving dishes; it makes for a nicer presentation. A hint on the vermouth: buy your wines for cooking and keep them for up to 2 months. They will lose taste for drinking, but are still great for cooking. A lot of people do not keep wine in the house for drinking, but would really love the flavor in cooking, so the way to do it is just keep a stock of two or three regular wines for cooking. NEVER USE COOKING WINE. It is very salty and will ruin your dishes.

Calories — 216; Carb — 18.2; Fat — 7.2; Chol — 100.0; Pro — 8.6; Fib — 1.1

SHRIMP FRED LAWRENCE

1/4 cup peanut oil
1/2 stick butter, unsalted
2 cloves garlic, minced
1 tsp. shallots, minced
2 tbsp. celery, minced
1 1/2 lb. medium shrimp (40-50 per lb.), peeled and deveined
1 medium sweet red bell pepper, cut into strips
1 medium green bell pepper, cut into strips
1 bunch green onions, chopped
1 large firm red tomato, diced
1/4 lb. oyster mushrooms, whole (or regular mushrooms sliced)

1/8 cup black olives, sliced
1/4 cup toasted walnuts, chopped coarsely
3 cups cooked white rice
1/2 cup fresh parsley, minced
1/4 cup dry vermouth
1 tsp. salt
1/4 tsp. Tabasco sauce
1 tsp. Worcestershire sauce
1 tsp. soy sauce
1/2 tsp. sweet basil
1/4 tsp. rosemary, crumbled

Heat a large, heavy skillet over high heat until hot. Add the peanut oil and when it starts to smoke, add the butter. As soon as the butter melts, add the garlic, shallots, and celery and sauté for 1 minute. Add the shrimp and sauté until they are pink throughout, about 3 minutes if your fire is hot enough. Add the red and green bell peppers and sauté for 30 seconds, then add the green onions and tomatoes; sauté for 1 minute. Add the mushrooms and olives, stirring them around until they are coated with the liquid. Add the walnuts, rice, and parsley and stir through until the rice is coated with the gravy. Add the wine and let it sizzle through; stir to blend. Add the remaining ingredients and mix in well. Remove from the heat and serve at once. Serves 8.

Lagniappe: This dish is hard to beat: low in calories and low in effort. Cut everything in advance because you won't be able to keep up with the dish once the pan is hot. Do not cook in advance, though, since it does not keep well. The taste stays fine, but the looks and texture are terrible after it sits. Total cooking time on this dish is under 8 minutes. You can really amaze your guests, family, and yourself with this dish. Have a blast; I do.

Calories—345; Carb—24.6; Fat—16.9; Chol—145.1; Pro—19.2; Fib—1.1

SCALLOPS BOURGEOIS

2 slices whole wheat light
   bread
1 lb. scallops
1/2 cup green onions,
   chopped
vegetable oil spray, butter
   flavor
2 tbsp. lemon juice
2 tbsp. diet margarine,
   melted
1 tbsp. white
   Worcestershire sauce
1/4 tsp. Tabasco sauce

2 tbsp. dry vermouth
3 tsp. Butter Buds
1 tsp. salt
1/2 tsp. cayenne pepper
1/2 tsp. sweet basil
1/2 tsp. garlic powder
1 tbsp. butter, unsalted
2 tbsp. fresh parsley,
   minced
12 fresh oyster
   mushrooms or regular
   mushrooms
paprika for garnish

Preheat the oven to 200 degrees. Place the 2 slices of bread in the oven and just leave them there until you are ready for them. Dry the scallops with paper towels, spray four individual baking shells or individual baking-serving dishes with the vegetable oil spray, and arrange one-fourth of the scallops and one-fourth of the green onions in each one of the dishes.

Mix together the lemon juice, margarine, Worcestershire, Tabasco, vermouth, and Butter Buds in a small saucepan and heat over low heat until hot. Spoon the liquid over the scallops equally. Mix together the salt, cayenne, sweet basil, and garlic powder, then sprinkle evenly over the scallops.

Change the temperature in the oven to broil and remove the bread from the oven. Break the bread into pieces, put it into a food processor, and make soft bread crumbs by turning on and leaving on until the bread has crumbled. Mix the bread crumbs, real butter, and parsley together by tossing. Chop the mushrooms coarsely and mix with the bread crumbs, then sprinkle it over the scallops. Garnish with the paprika and broil about 8 inches from the heat for 12 to 15 minutes or until the scallops are a puffy white color throughout. Serve right from the oven. Serves 4.

Lagniappe: The dish can be assembled completely for broiling and refrigerated until you are ready to broil. It will freeze fairly well after it has completely cooked. Just cover tightly with plastic wrap. To reheat, put into the microwave directly from the freezer and heat at 30 percent power for 1 minute, then change to 80 percent power for 2 minutes. To reheat without the microwave, just thaw in the refrigerator and bake at 300 degrees for 5 minutes or until hot. After the prep work is done on this dish, it is very easy to control heating time.

Calories — 151; Carb — 12.6; Fat — 6.9; Chol — 48.3; Pro — 20.6; Fib — 0.9

GARLIC-BASIL SHRIMP

2 tbsp. peanut oil
1 tbsp. butter, unsalted
5 large cloves garlic,
  chopped
1 tbsp. shallots, minced
1 tbsp. fresh sweet basil,
  minced (or use 1 tsp.
  dry)
1 1/3 lb. large shrimp,
  peeled and deveined

1 tsp. salt
1/2 tsp. fresh ground black
  pepper
1/4 tsp. Tabasco sauce
1/2 tsp. soy sauce
1/4 cup dry vermouth
1 tbsp. fresh lemon juice
1 tbsp. fresh parsley,
  minced
lemon wedges for garnish

In a large skillet over medium-high heat, add the peanut oil. When it is hot, add the butter and swirl it around until it melts. When it is hot, add the garlic and shallots and sauté for 2 minutes. Add the basil and shrimp; sauté until they are browned nicely on both sides, about 3 to 4 minutes. They will curl up and turn pink from head to tail. Add the salt, black pepper, Tabasco sauce, soy sauce, and vermouth. The wine should cause a bit of steam to come up. Stir well, then add the lemon juice, reduce the heat to low, and shake the pan a few times to prevent the shrimp from sticking. Add the parsley and stir through. Serve at once, garnished with lemon wedges. Serves 4.

Lagniappe: This is a fast dish and one that needs to be eaten right after cooking, so nothing can be done in advance but the peeling of the shrimp and the chopping of the garlic and shallots. This is a real crowd pleaser. If you keep shrimp in the freezer, you can do this dish almost at the drop of a hat. I suggest buying shrimp in 5-pound blocks from the seafood market or supermarket. Tell them you want it frozen. It is shaped so that you can run cold water on one end, just defrost what you need, then return the frozen part to the freezer. This way you always have fresh shrimp. When you see fresh shrimp at market, it is from the same once-frozen block! Shrimp frozen this way keeps a long time and is easy to use.

Calories — 265; Carb — 6.1; Fat — 8.4; Chol — 236.2; Pro — 29.5; Fib — 0.5

QUICK SHRIMP PASTA DINNER

1 lb. shrimp, peeled and deveined
1/4 tsp. red pepper
1/4 tsp. garlic powder
2 tbsp. butter, unsalted (or margarine)
1 clove garlic, minced
1 tsp. shallots, minced (not green onions)
8 large mushrooms, sliced
1 tbsp. brandy
1 tsp. fresh lemon juice
1/4 tsp. tarragon
1/2 tsp. sweet basil
1/4 tsp. white pepper
1/4 tsp. Tabasco sauce
1 tsp. salt
1/8 cup toasted slivered almonds
1 cup half-and-half cream
2 tbsp. fresh parsley, minced
2 cups cooked pasta, al dente

Season the shrimp with the red pepper and garlic powder. In a skillet over medium-high heat, melt the butter. When the butter begins to smoke, add the shrimp, garlic, shallots, and mushrooms; sauté until the shrimp are lightly browned on each side, about 1 minute each side. Remove from the heat and add in all the remaining ingredients except the pasta. Stir together well, reduce the heat to medium, and return the skillet to the stove. Simmer the mixture until the sauce becomes smooth and begins to thicken. Serve at once over the cooked pasta of your choice. Serves 4.

Lagniappe: This is such a quick dish that there is no reason to do it in advance. It should be eaten immediately after being cooked. Do not freeze. You can refrigerate after it is cooked, but the sauce may begin to separate.

If you are not counting calories, you can use 1 whole stick of butter to sauté the shrimp in, then substitute heavy cream for the half-and-half. This will give you a very rich and filling dish, but one that necessarily has more calories. You can also make the same dish with scallops, by substituting 1 pound of scallops for the 1 pound of shrimp to make **Quick Scallop Pasta Dinner.**

Calories — 388; Carb — 24.3; Fat — 16.9; Chol — 211.9; Pro — 28.2; Fib — 0.6

CATFISH FLORENTINE

1 1/2 tbsp. butter
4 8-oz. catfish fillets
1/8 cup dry vermouth
1 tbsp. fresh lemon juice
salt and pepper to taste
1/8 tsp. Tabasco sauce
1/4 tsp. tarragon
1/2 cup milk
4 oz. light cream cheese,
  chopped into chunks

1/2 tsp. salt
1/4 tsp. white pepper
1 lb. fresh spinach, cooked
  and chopped
2 tbsp. seasoned
  breadcrumbs
paprika for garnish
lemon slices for garnish
fresh parsley sprigs for
  garnish

Heat a large skillet over medium-high heat. Add the butter and let it melt. As it begins to smoke, quickly add the 4 catfish fillets. Brown them nicely on both sides, about 2 minutes each side. Add the vermouth, lemon juice, salt and pepper to taste, Tabasco, and tarragon and move the skillet around to let the flavors blend together. When the wine is reduced by half, about 1 minute, remove from the heat, cover with a lid, and set aside.

Preheat the broiler. In a medium saucepan over medium heat, add the milk, cream cheese, salt, and white pepper. Cook until the cream cheese is melted and blended into the milk. Mix this sauce with the spinach. Place each fish fillet on a serving platter that can take heat and pour the pan drippings equally onto each fillet. Spoon one-fourth of the spinach mixture on top of each catfish fillet. Now sprinkle with the seasoned breadcrumbs and paprika and place under broiler until lightly browned. Garnish with lemon slices and parsley sprigs. Serve at once. Serves 4.

Lagniappe: You can do part of this recipe in advance. Mix the spinach with the cream cheese sauce and have it ready to use, but the fish is so much better when eaten just after it is cooked. It can be made to the point of broiling, if time is really a big problem, but be prepared to lose some texture and taste. Do not freeze.

    It is also possible to use any number of different fish fillets in this dish. Two that I have tried are redfish to make **Redfish Floren-**

tine and red snapper to make **Red Snapper Florentine.**
Don't stop there; just use your favorite fish fillet and have at it!

Calories — 438; Carb — 9.7; Fat — 19.9; Chol — 104.9; Pro — 47.7; Fib — 0.9

TROUT MEUNIERE

vegetable oil spray
2 tbsp. diet margarine
4 6 oz. trout fillets, dried
   with paper towels
flour for dusting fish fillets
2 tbsp. butter, unsalted
1 tsp. shallots, minced (not
   green onions)
1 clove garlic, minced

1 tbsp. celery, chopped
1 tsp. flour
1/8 tsp. cayenne pepper
1/8 tsp. white pepper
1/2 tsp. salt
1/2 cup dry vermouth
1/4 cup chicken stock
2 tbsp. heavy cream
paprika for garnish

Spray a large skillet with the vegetable oil spray, then heat the pan over medium heat. Add the margarine and let it melt. Lightly coat the trout fillets with flour and when the margarine begins to smoke, fry the fillets for 4 minutes on each side. Remove to a warm platter for later use.

Add the butter to the skillet and when it melts, add the shallots, garlic, and celery and sauté for 3 minutes over medium heat. Add the flour, cayenne pepper, white pepper, and salt; sauté for 2 minutes, stirring constantly. Add the vermouth and chicken stock and blend in well. The sauce should thicken somewhat. Remove from the heat, lower the temperature to low, and add the cream. Blend in well and return to the heat; cook until it thickens somewhat. Add the parsley and stir in. Arrange each fillet on a warm serving plate and spoon the meunière sauce equally over each. Sprinkle with paprika and serve. Serves 4.

Lagniappe: This dish cannot be made in advance, but the cooking time
   is short and should not be a problem. This meunière lends itself to
   other fish and can be made in the same way, just substituting the fish
   fillets of your choice. Enjoy!

Calories — 310; Carb — 2.4; Fat — 15.8; Chol — 121.4; Pro — 33.9; Fib — Trace

BAKED SALMON SAUCE DIJON

4 steaks salmon, about 5 oz. each and 1-inch thick
1/2 tsp. salt
1/2 tsp. red pepper
1/2 tsp. garlic powder
1/4 tsp. tarragon

vegetable oil spray, butter flavor
3 tbsp. dry white wine
1 tbsp. fresh lime juice
1 1/4 cup Sauce Dijon (see index for recipe)

Preheat the oven to 350 degrees. Wash the salmon steaks under cold water, then pat them dry with paper towels. Mix together the seasonings until they are well blended. Spray a baking dish large enough to hold the 4 steaks with the vegetable oil spray and arrange the salmon steaks in the pan. Mix together the wine and lime juice and spoon over the salmon equally. Sprinkle half of the seasoning mixture on top of the salmon; reserve the rest.

Cover and bake at 350 degrees for 20 minutes. The fish should flake easily when tested with a fork. Remove from the pan and turn over onto four warm serving plates. Season the salmon again with the reserved seasoning mixture. Spoon 2 1/2 tablespoons of sauce over each fish or serve on the side in a sauce boat or bowl. Serves 4.

Lagniappe: This is a real treat! Fresh salmon steaks are now available in most major supermarkets or in fresh seafood markets. Salmon lends itself to delicate saucing and relatively short cooking times. Enjoy!

Do not make your Sauce Dijon in advance. This recipe is simple, and you can use the Light Butter Sauce (see index for recipe) instead of the Sauce Dijon and make **Baked Salmon With Light Butter Sauce.** Just substitute the Butter Sauce for the Sauce Dijon. Hollandaise Light also is quite nice with salmon.

BAKED SALMON WITHOUT SAUCE: Calories — 327; Carb — 1.2; Fat — 19.4; Chol — 50.0; Pro — 32.3; Fib — 0.1

WITH 2 TABLESPOONS OF SAUCE: Calories — 407; Carb — 5.0; Fat — 20.2; Chol — 104.8; Pro — 33.9; Fib — 0.2

GRILLED FOIL FISH

4 tbsp. diet margarine
4 fillets (8 oz. each) fish of
  your choice
salt, black and red pepper
  to taste
2 tbsp. Worcestershire
  sauce

2 tbsp. fresh lemon juice
8 large mushrooms, sliced
2 cloves garlic, minced
2 tsp. shallots, minced
3 tsp. Butter Buds
1 tsp. tarragon
1 tsp. sweet basil

Soften the margarine and rub 1 tablespoon on each of the 4 fish fillets. Tear out 4 long pieces of foil so that each one is 3 1/2 times the length of the fish fillet. Fold the foil in half and place a fillet in the center of each piece of foil. Season with salt and black and red pepper. Spoon 1/2 tablespoon of both Worcestershire sauce and fresh lemon juice over each fish; fold the sides of the foil up to prevent the liquid from running off. Arrange the slices from two mushrooms over each fillet. Sprinkle equally with garlic, shallots, Butter Buds, tarragon, and basil.

Fold the foil tightly closed and place on a gas or charcoal grill. Close the lid to allow the fish to cook from all sides. Grill for 20 minutes or until the fish begins to flake when you run a knife on the top of the fillet. Serve hot in the foil packet. Serves 4.

Lagniappe: This is a simple and delicious fish grill that is a refreshing change from grilled meat. Do not cook in advance, but you can prepare the fish in the foil for grilling and refrigerate until you are ready to cook. Simply thaw in the refrigerator and cook as above. This makes the grilling no chore at all. It is really nice to have something in the freezer that you can get to quickly should the "unexpected" arrive. I like to prepare 8 to 12 foil packets of fish fillets whenever I get too much fresh fish to eat at one time. After the foil packets are closed, put 4 fillet foil packets into a large plastic freezer bag and close tightly; this will help to protect your fish fillets even longer.

Calories — 316; Carb — 5.7; Fat — 8.1; Chol — 125.7; Pro — 45.5; Fib — 0.6

SOLE ROLL WITH
HOLLANDAISE LIGHT

2 lb. fillet of sole, boned
2 tbsp. lemon juice
1 tsp. salt
1/2 tsp. cayenne pepper
1 1/4 tsp. paprika
1/2 tsp. sweet basil
1/4 tsp. tarragon
1/4 tsp. white pepper
1/2 tsp. garlic powder
3 Shiitake mushrooms,
    minced
1 tsp. shallots, minced
1 tbsp. parsley, minced
2 cups dry white wine

2 cups chicken stock or
    chicken broth (or
    seafood stock)
6 whole green pepper-
    corns
6 whole black peppercorns
3 whole cloves
1/4 cup green onions,
    chopped
1/4 cup carrots, minced
1 clove garlic, crushed
1 cup Hollandaise Light
    (see index for recipe)
lemon wedges for garnish

Wash each fillet of sole under cold water and dry with paper towel. Lay on a cutting board and cut into strips about 2 inches wide and 7 inches long. Sprinkle evenly with the lemon juice. Mix together the salt, cayenne pepper, paprika, basil, tarragon, white pepper, and garlic powder. Season each strip of sole with the seasoning mixture. Mix together the mushrooms, shallots, and parsley. Spoon a small amount of the mushroom mixture onto the smallest end of each strip. Starting with that end, roll the strips into tight round rolls, with the seasoned sides in the center. Fasten with a toothpick (do not use plastic). Repeat the process until all rolls are done. Set the rolls in the refrigerator until you are ready to serve. Place in either a poacher or a deep non-aluminum pot. Add all the remaining ingredients, except for the sauce, to the pan and bring to a boil. Once the liquid begins to boil, reduce to simmer and simmer for 15 minutes. Add the sole rolls, cover, and poach over simmer for 5 minutes. Test with a fork, and if the fish flakes, carefully remove from the pan. Sauce with Hollandaise Light and garnish with lemon wedges. Serves 6.

Lagniappe: As you can see, cooking time is very short, so there is no problem with cooking right before you eat. You can make the rolls up to 48 hours in advance and keep refrigerated until ready to poach. Do not cook and refrigerate. You can also simmer your poaching sauce ahead of time and all you need do is bring it to a simmer and add the fish. The simmering of the poaching liquid helps to bring the flavors together. If you like, you can choose another sauce from the sauce section.

WITH 3 TABLESPOONS OF SAUCE: Calories — 200; Carb — 12.6; Fat — 2.7; Chol — 195.6; Pro — 25.6; Fib — 0.4

WINE-POACHED TROUT

2 1/4 cups dry white wine
2 1/4 cups chicken stock or chicken broth
1 cup carrots, sliced
1/2 cup celery, chopped
2/3 cup green onions, chopped
3 sprigs parsley
1/8 tsp. tarragon
1/4 tsp. sweet basil
1/4 tsp. thyme
1 clove garlic, whole
1 whole clove
1 large bay leaf
1 tsp. salt
5 green peppercorns, crushed
4 black peppercorns, crushed
4 whole (1 lb. each) trout, cleaned
2 tbsp. cornstarch
2 tbsp. cold water
1 tsp. tarragon vinegar
2 tsp. fresh lemon juice
1 packet (1/2 oz.) Butter Buds
1 tbsp. fresh parsley, minced
paprika for garnish
lemon wedges for garnish

Put all the ingredients but the last nine (up to the trout) into a large skillet or into a fish poacher. Bring to a boil and boil for 1 minute, then reduce to a simmer. Simmer uncovered for 45 minutes. Add all the trout and poach for 10 minutes at a low simmer, making sure that the liquid covers the whole fish. When poached, carefully remove the fish to a warm serving platter and set aside for later use.

Use a wire strainer and strain the broth into a small saucepan. Cook the broth over medium heat until it is reduced by half. Mix together the cornstarch, cold water, tarragon vinegar, and lemon juice and stir until the cornstarch is dissolved. Mix the cornstarch liquid into the hot saucepan and return to medium heat until the sauce thickens. Add the Butter Buds and the fresh minced teaspoon of parsley and, using a wire whisk, stir until the sauce is smooth. Place each trout on a warm serving plate and spoon a generous amount of sauce on top of the fish. Garnish with paprika and lemon wedges. Serve at once. Serves 4.

Lagniappe: You cannot make this dish in advance or freeze. You can do all your preparation and make your poaching liquid and refrigerate until you are ready to poach the fish. Do not attempt to poach the fish and make the sauce in advance, or you will be disappointed and not really give the dish a fair chance. This is company eating, but easy enough for everyday fare.

Calories — 480; Carb — 7.1; Fat — 2.7; Chol — 253.9; Pro — 90.9; Fib — Trace

SHRIMP CREOLE DANIELLE

1/4 cup corn oil
2 large yellow onions,
  chopped
1 large bell pepper,
  coarsely chopped
1 medium sweet red bell
  pepper, chopped
1 cup celery, chopped
3 cloves garlic, minced
2 cups stewed tomatoes
1 tsp. salt
1 tbsp. paprika
1 tbsp. Tabasco sauce

1 tbsp. Worcestershire
  sauce
1/2 tsp. black pepper
1/2 tsp. filé powder
1/2 tsp. sweet basil
1 large bay leaf
1 cup warm water
2 1/4 lb. medium shrimp
  (40-50 per lb.), peeled
  and deveined
1/4 cup cold water
2 tbsp. cornstarch
4 cups cooked white rice

Heat the oil in a large saucepan over medium heat until it is hot. Add the onions, bell pepper, red bell pepper, celery, and garlic. Sauté until all the vegetables are limp and the onions are clear, about 5 minutes. Add the tomatoes and continue to sauté until the tomatoes begin to dissolve, about 5 more minutes. Add the salt, paprika, Tabasco sauce, Worcestershire sauce, black pepper, filé, sweet basil, and bay leaf. Mix in well. Add the warm water and reduce the heat to simmer; simmer for 20 minutes. Add the shrimp and simmer for 10 minutes. Dissolve the cornstarch in the cold water, add to the saucepan, and stir in well. The sauce should thicken quickly. Serve at once over 1/2 cup cooked white rice for each serving. Serves 8.

Lagniappe: You can freeze or refrigerate this dish for later use. Do not add the cornstarch before refrigerating or freezing. To serve, just thaw in the refrigerator and return to a saucepan at simmer. Add the cornstarch-water mixture when the sauce begins to bubble. This is both easy and tasty, a real winner.

Calories — 325; Carb — 35.0; Fat — 8.2; Chol — 192.9; Pro — 27.6; Fib — 1.3

AUNT LILI BELLE'S
SPICY HOT CRAB

1 lb. lump crabmeat
1/2 tsp. salt
1/2 tsp. cayenne pepper
1/4 tsp. white pepper
1 tbsp. peanut oil
2 cloves garlic, minced
1/4 cup celery, minced
1 medium onion, sliced
1/2 cup green bell pepper, diced
1 cup chicken stock or chicken broth
3 tbsp. soy sauce

1 cup broccoli florets
6 large mushrooms, sliced
1 cup frozen sweet green peas, thawed
1/4 cup cold water
1 tbsp. cornstarch
1 tbsp. dry sherry
1 tbsp. fresh ginger, minced
1 tsp. sugar
1/2 tsp. dry hot mustard
1/4 tsp. Tabasco sauce
2 cups cooked white rice

Sprinkle the crabmeat with the salt and peppers. Heat a large skillet over medium heat until it is hot, then add the peanut oil. When the oil starts to smoke, add the seasoned crabmeat and garlic and sauté carefully for 2 minutes. Remove to a warm platter for later use. Add the onions, celery, and bell pepper and sauté for 3 minutes; there won't be much oil left but there will be enough. Add the chicken stock and soy sauce and bring to a boil. When it begins to boil, reduce to a simmer and add the broccoli, mushrooms, and peas. Simmer for 8 minutes.

Mix together the cold water, cornstarch, and sherry until the cornstarch is dissolved and pour into the chicken stock-vegetable mix when the 8 minutes are up. Let the sauce thicken, then add the fresh ginger, sugar, hot mustard, and Tabasco. Mix in well. Fold in the rice and the warm crabmeat until mixed. Serve hot. Serves 6.

Lagniappe: This dish is best eaten right after cooking. You can refrigerate and serve later, but you lose so much of the freshness and color of the dish. I suggest that you only cut up your vegetables and get everything ready to cook, then cook right before dinner.

You can use the same recipe to make **Aunt Lili Belle's Spicy Hot Shrimp** with just a few easy substitutions. Use 1 1/4 pound of shrimp instead of crabmeat. You will need to increase the cooking time from 2 minutes for the crab to 3 1/2 minutes for the shrimp. Everything else remains the same. Bon appetit!

Calories — 225; Carb — 25.4; Fat — 4.4; Chol — 76.9; Pro — 18.5; Fib — 1.3

Meats

The first thing I want to mention about meats is a word of caution. Most of us eat too much meat, red meat in particular. Americans eat more than their own weight per year in red meat on the average. We need to change this habit and eat more seafood and poultry.

Now that this is out of the way, let's talk about meat itself. The best way to cut calories when eating meats is to eat lean meat. The second way is to control portions very carefully. Both are easy to do. Use the exact measurements listed and follow the directions. You will find there are many low-calorie meals possible with meat. I still like to limit red meat to no more than two meals a week. That is not easy at first, but try it and you may be adding years to your life.

When you shop for meat, look for lean cuts. Heavy beef or prime beef may taste better, but those grades are loaded with extra saturated fats. It is choice time. I am not going to say not to eat them; if you do, just be sure to count your calories. If you are going to eat about 1,500 to 2,000 calories per day, that doesn't leave much room for prime beef. If you want a tender piece of beef, choose the tenderloin. It is very tender and low in fat content. It may be expensive but the cost per serving is fairly reasonable. You get fewer calories, as well as great quality and taste. What more can you ask for? Pork tenderloin has similar advantages.

Generally, ground chuck or ground round are lower in calories and fat. You would do better to buy a chuck roast or round steak and then bring it home and grind it yourself. Veal is, in most cases, much lower in calories than beef or pork, but that is not always true. Be sure to buy the exact piece of meat the recipe calls for, to insure that the calorie count is accurate.

You can now buy turkey or chicken sausage in most markets. This lowers calories, fat, and cholesterol significantly. The taste is so close to the original that you will be amazed. The spices and smoking help to make the product excellent.

The best advice to leave you with is stick to the cuts and quantities recommended. If you alter a recipe, be sure to do an accurate calorie count yourself. Meats are fun to cook with, but if you are seriously counting your calories, eat them with caution.

SUKIYAKI

2 tbsp. peanut oil
1 1/4 lb. boneless beef
  round steak, cut into
  thin strips
1 bunch green onions, cut
  into 2-inch diagonal
  pieces
2 tbsp. soy sauce
6 large mushrooms, sliced
1 cup celery, cut into
  1-inch diagonal pieces
1/2 cup bell pepper,
  coarsely cut
1/4 cup toasted slivered
  almonds

1 can (6 oz.) bamboo
  shoots, drained and cut
  into fourths
1 cup snow pea pods
1/2 cup beef stock or beef
  broth
2 tsp. cornstarch
1/4 tsp. Tabasco sauce
1/4 tsp. garlic powder
1 tbsp. sugar
1/4 tsp. sweet basil
1/4 tsp. fresh grated
  ginger
1/2 tsp. salt
3 cups cooked white rice

Heat a large skillet over high heat until hot. Add the peanut oil and bring it to the smoking point. Add the round steak and green onions and sauté over high heat for 2 1/2 minutes. Move the beef-green onion mixture to one side of the skillet and sprinkle with the soy sauce. Add the mushrooms, celery, bell pepper, bamboo shoots, almonds, and snow peas. Sauté for 2 minutes, stirring often. Mix the beef stock with the cornstarch and stir until the cornstarch is dissolved. Add the cornstarch-beef stock mixture and all the remaining ingredients except for the rice and bring to a boil. As soon as it boils, reduce to a simmer, cover, and simmer for 7 minutes, stirring a few times during the cooking process. Serve hot over the cooked white rice. Serves 6.

Lagniappe: You can make this dish in advance and refrigerate until you are ready to serve, but you do loose some of the vegetables' crispness. It is still quite good. Just cook over a low fire until heated through and serve.

You can make **Chicken Sukiyaki** by substituting 1 1/4 pounds of chicken breast cut into bite-size pieces for the beef steak. Cook exactly as above except use chicken stock for the beef stock. It makes a nice alternative to beef.

Calories — 446; Carb — 32.7; Fat — 20.2; Chol — 76.7; Pro — 37.5; Fib — 1.5

PORK CHOPS KATHLEEN

6 8 oz. center cut pork chops, about 1/2-inch thick
1 tbsp. peanut oil
1/2 cup chicken stock or chicken broth
3 tbsp. cream sherry
1 tbsp. Worcestershire sauce
1 tbsp. soy sauce
2 tsp. shallots (not green onions)
2 cloves garlic, minced
1/2 tsp. fresh grated ginger
1/2 cup celery, cut into 1/2-inch diagonal pieces
1/4 cup snow pea pods, cleaned and stems removed

1 can (6 oz.) water chestnuts, sliced
3/4 cup bell pepper, coarsely chopped
1/2 cup green onions, chopped 1 inch thick
1 cup broccoli florets
1/2 cup bok choy, chopped
2 tsp. cornstarch
1/8 cup cold water
1/4 tsp. Tabasco sauce
1 tbsp. lemon juice
1 tsp. salt
1/4 tsp. white pepper
1/4 tsp. sweet basil
1/4 tsp. Beau Monde seasoning
3 cups cooked white rice or noodles

Heat a large skillet with a cover over medium-high heat until hot. Add the peanut oil and when it begins to smoke, add the chops and brown well on both sides. Add the chicken stock, cream sherry, Worcestershire sauce, soy sauce, shallots, garlic, and ginger; bring to a boil, then reduce the heat to simmer. Cover and simmer the chops until they are tender, about 20 minutes; make sure that your chops are thoroughly cooked.

Remove the chops from the pan to a warm platter, cover, and keep warm. Add the vegetables, raise the temperature, and bring to a full boil. Stir the vegetables frequently and cook for 2 minutes. Reduce the heat to low and cover; cook for 2 minutes without stirring. Mix the cornstarch with the cold water and add with the rest of the ingredients, except for the rice, to the cooked vegetables; stir in well.

Return the chops to the pan and cover them with the vegetables and liquid. Cover and simmer over low for 2 to 3 more minutes until the sauce is somewhat thickened and the chops heated through. Serve at once over cooked white rice or noodles. Serves 6.

Lagniappe: This can be made in advance and reheated, but do not freeze. Refrigerate until ready to use (it will keep for about 3 days); keep tightly covered. I suggest stopping the cooking right at the point of returning the chops to the skillet. Simply put the chops in a dish that can be covered, pour the vegetable mixture over the top, cover, and refrigerate. When ready to heat, pour into the skillet, cover, and simmer over low for 4 to 5 minutes until heated through. Do remember that any dish with as much fresh vegetables as this dish has is always going to be better when first cooked. This is basically a one-dish meal. All that is needed to complement the meal is either a crisp salad or a couple of slices of chilled melon.

Calories — 545; Carb — 34.8; Fat — 21.9; Chol — 120.0; Pro — 63.9; Fib — 1.1

STEAK AND MUSHROOM
SHISH KEBABS

1/2 cup hearty burgundy
  wine
3 tbsp. Worcestershire
  sauce
1 tsp. Tabasco sauce
2 cloves garlic, minced
1 tsp. shallot, minced
1 tbsp. vegetable oil
2 tsp. sugar
2 tbsp. fresh lemon juice
2 tbsp. red wine vinegar
1 tsp. fresh rosemary,
  crushed (or 1/2 tsp. dry)

1/2 tsp. salt
1/2 tsp. fresh sweet basil,
  crushed (or 1/4 tsp. dry)
1/4 tsp. marjoram
1/4 tsp. fresh ground black
  pepper
12 large mushrooms,
  stems removed
1 large sweet red bell
  pepper, cut into large
  pieces
1 lb. sirloin steak

In a large bowl, mix together all but the last three ingredients. Wash the mushrooms to remove all grit. Add the mushrooms and the red pepper pieces to the bowl. Cut the steak into 1 1/2-inch cubes and add them to the bowl. There should be enough liquid to cover the steak, pepper, and mushrooms (the mushrooms may float at times until they get some of the liquid absorbed). Let the mixture marinate overnight.

Alternate steak, mushroom cap, and red bell pepper on each of four skewers until all is used. Broil in the oven or on a gas grill, turning the shish kebabs often to brown all sides. Baste often with the marinade. Serve hot. Serves 4.

Lagniappe: No need to worry about refrigerating on this recipe; you have to! You can even let the kebabs marinate for up to 3 days. Cooking time is short and this is a lot of fun. Serve with rice or potatoes for an excellent, easy dish.

Calories — 394; Carb — 10.7; Fat — 18.9; Chol — 92.0; Pro — 38.9; Fib — 1.0

GRILLED MINTED
LAMB CHOPS PAULIN

**4 chops (5 oz. each) lamb,
lean and cut about
3/4-inch thick**
**1 tbsp. green crème de
menthe liqueur**
2 tbsp. fresh lime juice
**2 tbsp. fresh mint leaves,
chopped**

**1 tsp. white Worces-
tershire sauce**
1 tbsp. red wine vinegar
1 tsp. salt
1/2 tsp. garlic powder
1/2 tsp. shallots, minced
**fresh sprigs of mint for
garnish**

Trim the chops of any excess fat and use a fork to make a number of punctures in the chops. Mix together the remaining ingredients, except for the garnish, and blend well. Place the chops in a shallow dish and pour the marinade over them. Cover and refrigerate for at least 4 hours, turning at least 5 times during the marinating. When you are ready to serve, grill the chops over hot coals until nicely browned on each side, but still pink and juicy in the center, about 4 to 5 minutes per side. Baste constantly with the marinade while grilling. Serve at once, and garnish with fresh mint sprigs if you like. Serves 4.

Lagniappe: You can't cook in advance of serving, but you can marinate for up to 2 days. That should give you all the leeway you need. Be sure to find a good source of lamb chops in your area, well before you decide to serve. Most large supermarkets will even cut the chops to your specifications.

Calories — 280; Carb — 3.8; Fat — 13.6; Chol — 87.0; Pro — 25.2; Fib — Trace

PORK CHOPS BRANDIED FLAMBE

4 large 10-oz. center cut
  pork chops, with extra
  fat trimmed
1/2 tsp. cayenne pepper
1/2 tsp. black pepper
1/2 tsp. white pepper
1 tsp. salt
1 tsp. onion powder
1 tsp. garlic powder
1/4 tsp. sweet basil

1/4 tsp. dry hot mustard
2 medium white onions,
  sliced 1/4-inch thick and
  separated into rings
2 cloves garlic, minced
1 tbsp. olive oil
2 tbsp. butter or margarine
1/4 cup brandy
1 tbsp. fresh parsley,
  chopped

Take the pork chops and pound them a few times with a kitchen mallet. Mix together all the dry seasonings until well blended. Equally season both sides of each chop, pressing some of the seasoning into the chop. Place the chops in a container large enough to hold all four side by side and cover with the onion rings and garlic. Sprinkle the remaining seasoning on top of the onions. Tightly cover and let the chops sit in the refrigerator overnight or at least 8 hours.

When you are ready to cook, heat a large, heavy skillet over medium-high heat until hot. Add the olive oil and butter; let the butter melt. When the butter starts to smoke, add the chops to the skillet and cover with the onions and garlic. Brown on the first side for 4 minutes, then turn the chops over and cook for another 4 minutes.

Reduce the temperature to low and carefully add the brandy. Strike a match and bring it carefully to the skillet; there will be a puff and a strong fire. BE CAREFUL! If you are not used to working with flambés, you may want to watch someone cook this first. Do not shake the pan or stir; the flame will go out naturally. When it does, turn the chops over, stir the onions around, cover, and cook over low for 10 minutes. Remove the cover, stir well, add the parsley, and serve at once. Serves 4.

Lagniappe: Cooking time is very short, and this is truly a dish you will
  want to prepare in front of your family or guests. Please do be

cautious with the flambé. You can refrigerate the seasoned chops for up to 3 days; it will actually improve the flavor as the seasonings blend through more. Serve with a plain baked potato or a rice dish and a green vegetable. This is a simple but divine dish.

Calories — 489; Carb — 6.6; Fat — 25.7; Chol — 100.0; Pro — 50.8; Fib — 0.6

VEAL CHOPS MELINE

4 chops veal, about 3 1/2 oz. each
1 tbsp. all-purpose flour
1/2 tsp. salt
1/4 tsp. red pepper
1/4 tsp. white pepper
1/4 tsp. onion powder
1/4 tsp. garlic powder
vegetable oil spray, butter flavor
1 1/2 tbsp. butter, unsalted (or margarine)
1 tsp. shallots, minced

8 medium Shiitake mushrooms
4 large mushrooms, thinly sliced
1/4 cup lean ham, diced
2 tbsp. Cognac
1/4 cup beef stock or beef broth
1/4 cup sweet red bell pepper, cut into strips
1 tbsp. capers
2 tbsp. fresh parsley
1/4 tsp. Tabasco sauce

Remove any fat from the veal chops. Mix together well the flour, salt, red pepper, white pepper, onion powder, and garlic powder. Spray a heavy skillet with the vegetable oil spray and place over medium heat until hot. Add the butter and let it melt.

As the butter is melting, lightly coat the chops with the seasoned flour. The butter should be smoking when you finish; quickly add the flour-coated chops to the skillet. Fry for 2 minutes on the first side, then turn the veal over and fry for 2 1/2 minutes. Turn the veal over and fry for 2 more minutes on the first side. Don't alter this set of instructions. Remove to a warm plate and add the shallots, Shiitake mushrooms, mushrooms, and ham. Sauté for 2 to 3 minutes, then add the Cognac. Stir around and shake the pan for a second, then flambé by lighting with a match. There will be a puff and a very hot flame, but it will only last for a short time. BE CAREFUL! Add the beef stock. Deglaze the pan by dissolving the dark particles on the pan surface into the liquid. Add the remaining ingredients and cook for about 2 more minutes, stirring constantly. Arrange the veal chops on four plates and spoon the vegetable-ham mixture equally on top of each chop. Spoon the pan liquid on top of the vegetables and serve at once. Serves 4.

Lagniappe: This dish is easy, easy, easy . . . I've gone and done it again. Total cooking time is under 8 minutes. Read through once and you'll see that this is very simple. Just a reminder: do not dredge the veal in the seasoned flour in advance of the cooking. It will make the flour dusting turn to a heavy batter. Do not make in advance and, of course, you cannot freeze this dish.

Calories — 390; Carb — 4.9; Fat — 21.6; Chol — 108.9; Pro — 39.7; Fib — 0.7

BAKED PORK CHOPS MANUEL

6 center cut lean pork
  chops, about 5 oz. each
1 tsp. salt
1/2 tsp. red pepper
1/2 tsp. white pepper
1/2 tsp. garlic powder
vegetable oil spray, butter
  flavor
1 large onion, chopped
1 large green bell pepper,
  cut into thin strips
1 large sweet red bell
  pepper, cut into thin
  strips

3 cloves garlic, minced
2 tbsp. celery, minced
2 cups stewed tomatoes
1/4 tsp. Tabasco sauce
1 tbsp. Worcestershire
  sauce
2 tbsp. extra dry vermouth
1 tsp. sweet basil
1/2 tsp. oregano
1/4 tsp. rosemary
2 tbsp. fresh parsley,
  minced
2 tbsp. cold water

Season the pork chops evenly with the salt, peppers, and garlic powder. Press the seasonings into the meat with your fingers. Set the meat aside for later use.

In a small skillet over medium-high heat, spray the bottom with the vegetable oil spray. When the skillet is hot add the onion, green and red pepper, garlic, and celery. Sauté for 2 minutes, constantly stirring. Add the stewed tomatoes and sauté for 2 more minutes. Reduce the heat to simmer and add the Tabasco, Worcestershire sauce, vermouth, basil, oregano, and rosemary; simmer uncovered for 5 minutes. Add the parsley, mix in well, and continue to simmer until the chops are ready.

Preheat the oven to 350 degrees before you begin to cook the chops. In a large, heavy skillet over medium heat, add the seasoned chops and the cold water. Cook until the water has evaporated and the chops brown well on one side; they will start sizzling. Turn them over and brown well on the other side. Remove them and drain on a few paper towels, which will remove any excess oil.

Arrange the chops in a shallow 2 1/2- to 3-quart casserole that has a tight-fitting cover. Pour the tomato sauce over the chops and bake at 350 degrees for 45 to 50 minutes, covered. Remove the cover and continue to bake for 25 minutes, which should make the chops very tender. Serve hot with plenty of tomato sauce. Serves 6.

Lagniappe: This is a great make-ahead dish. You can either completely cook and refrigerate or cook for the 45 to 50 minutes, wrap tightly with plastic wrap, and freeze for later use. If you refrigerate, just heat at about 300 degrees for 15 minutes or until hot. If you freeze, just defrost in the refrigerator and bake at 350 degrees for the 25 minutes as above. Why the difference, you may ask? We want the extra liquid for freezing, so we do not cook completely before freezing. This is great for company or just everyday cooking for the family.

Calories — 320; Carb — 8.7; Fat — 10.1; Chol — 70.0; Pro — 31.7; Fib — 1.2

LAMB CHOPS EMAS

vegetable oil spray, butter
  flavor
1 tsp. olive oil
4 medium lean lamb
  chops, about 5 oz. each
1 tsp. salt
1/2 tsp. cayenne pepper
1/2 tsp. onion powder
1/4 tsp. dried sage
1/2 cup onions, chopped
2 cloves garlic, minced

4 large mushrooms, thinly
  sliced
1 cup beef stock or beef
  broth
1 tsp. white
  Worcestershire sauce
2 tsp. arrowroot
1/4 tsp. Tabasco sauce
2 tsp. Butter Buds
1 tsp. red wine vinegar

Trim any excess fat from the lamb chops. Spray a heavy nonstick skillet with the vegetable oil spray and add the olive oil. Heat over medium heat until the pan is hot and the oil begins to smoke. Add the chops and cook for 5 minutes on the first side and about 4 minutes on the second side. Remove and drain the chops on paper towels, and season with salt, cayenne, onion powder, and sage.

Wipe the pan clean with another paper towel to remove any remaining oil. Spray again with the vegetable oil spray and when the pan is again hot, add the onions, garlic, and mushroom. Sauté until the onions have nicely browned, about 3 to 4 minutes.

Mix the arrowroot with the beef stock and Worcestershire sauce, then stir until it is dissolved. Add the stock to the onion-sauté mixture. Stir in well. Add the remaining ingredients, stir well, then bring the mixture to a boil. Reduce the heat to simmer, add the browned chops, and simmer for 5 to 7 minutes or until the sauce is well thickened. Serve hot with plenty of the sauce. Serves 4.

Lagniappe: Don't do this recipe in advance. The lamb will lose its
  flavor and juice. There is not a lot of detailed work to this recipe, so
  you can be doing other activities while the lamb is simmering. Most
  supermarkets have meat departments that carry lamb and will cut it
  to your needs. Talk to your butcher.

*Calories — 186; Carb — 3.8; Fat — 15.2; Chol — 70.0; Pro — 32.0; Fib —
0.5*

VEAL AND MUSHROOMS

1 1/2 lb. veal sirloin steak, cut into strips
1 tbsp. flour
1 1/2 tbsp. butter or margarine
1 tsp. salt
1/2 tsp. black pepper
1/4 tsp. cayenne pepper
1 large yellow onion, chopped
1 clove garlic, minced
1 bay leaf
1/2 tsp. thyme
1/4 tsp. sweet basil
1 cup hearty burgundy wine
1/2 cup beef stock or beef broth
9 large mushrooms, sliced
1/4 tsp. Tabasco sauce
1 tbsp. fresh parsley, minced
cooked white rice

Heat a large, heavy skillet over medium heat until hot. Flour the veal strips evenly, using the tablespoon of flour. All flour should be used. When the pan is hot, add the butter and let it melt. When the butter starts to smoke but not brown, add the veal and sauté until well browned on all sides. Add the salt, black pepper, and cayenne pepper to the meat as evenly as possible, then add the onion and garlic; sauté for 1 minute. Add the bay leaf, thyme, basil, wine, and beef stock and bring to a boil, then reduce to a low simmer and cook for 15 minutes. Stir often. Add the mushrooms and Tabasco sauce and continue to simmer for 15 more minutes, stirring a few more times during the cooking process. Add the parsley and stir in well, then serve at once over the cooked white rice. Serves 6.

Lagniappe: This dish can be made in advance and either frozen or refrigerated for later use. Just defrost in the refrigerator and add to a pan over low heat and simmer until heated through. It can also be reheated in the microwave; just cover with plastic wrap (don't forget to punch a few holes in the wrap to let steam escape) and heat at full power for about 2 minutes. If you want the gravy to be a little thicker, you can use either arrowroot or cornstarch dissolved in a little cold water as a thickener.

Calories—400; Carb—5.7; Fat—20.5; Chol—111.3; Pro—39.3; Fib—0.5

TENDERLOIN OF PORK OLIVIA

1 lb. pork tenderloin, cut
   into 8 equal slices
1 tsp. salt
1/2 tsp. cayenne pepper
1/4 tsp. white pepper
1/8 tsp. celery seed
1/8 tsp. cilantro
1/4 tsp. garlic powder
vegetable oil spray, butter
   flavor
1 tbsp. butter, unsalted (or
   margarine)
1 cup green onions,
   chopped
1 cup mushrooms, thinly
   sliced
1/2 cup chicken stock or
   chicken broth
1/4 cup dry white wine
2 tbsp. Dijon mustard
1/4 tsp. Tabasco sauce
1 tsp. paprika
1 tbsp. fresh parsley,
   minced
1/2 cup plain yogurt,
   low-fat

Cut any excess fat from the tenderloin slices. Mix together the salt, cayenne pepper, white pepper, celery seed, cilantro, and garlic powder. Equally season each of the slices of pork. Use your fingers to push the seasoning into the meat. Spray a heavy nonstick skillet with the vegetable oil spray and heat over medium heat. When hot, add the butter and let it melt.

When the butter begins to smoke, quickly add each slice of pork and sauté for 5 minutes on each side. Remove the pork and set in a warm platter for later use. Add the green onions and mushrooms and sauté them for 3 minutes. Add the chicken stock, white wine, Dijon mustard, and Tabasco and stir in well. Add the pork to the skillet, reduce the heat to simmer, and simmer for 10 minutes. Add the paprika and parsley and simmer together for 10 more minutes.

Remove the pork and keep warm on a serving platter. Add the yogurt to the liquid and blend. Let the sauce simmer for 3 minutes, but do not let it boil or the yogurt will separate. Spoon the sauce over the pork and serve at once. Serves 4.

Lagniappe: This dish must be made just before eating. It is elegant, tasty, and not really difficult. The bulk of your time is spent simmering the flavors together. You have time to prepare whatever you are serving with this dish while the pork is simmering. I like a nice colorful vegetable to complement, and just a plain boiled potato or cup of some type of noodle as the starch.

Calories — 361; Carb — 10.8; Fat — 18.9; Chol — 90.5; Pro — 38.9; Fib — 0.7

PEPPER STEAK

2 lb. sirloin steak,
  about 1 inch thick
1/2 tsp. cayenne pepper
1 tsp. salt
1/2 tsp. garlic powder
1/4 cup peanut oil
2 tsp. shallots, minced
3 cloves garlic, minced
1 tsp. fresh grated ginger
1/4 cup celery, sliced into
  1/2-inch pieces
2 large green peppers, cut
  into strips 1/4-inch thick
1 large sweet red pepper,
  cut into strips 1/4-inch
  thick
2 large onions, cut into
  thin strips

1 can (6 oz.) water
  chestnuts, sliced
1/4 cup soy sauce
1/2 cup beef stock or beef
  broth
1/4 cup hearty burgundy
  wine
1 tbsp. Worcestershire
  sauce
1 tsp. sugar
1/4 tsp. Tabasco sauce
1 1/2 tbsp. cornstarch
1/4 cup cold water
1 cup green onions,
  chopped
1/4 cup parsley, minced
cooked white rice

Place the steak in the freezer and let it freeze lightly, which will aid in cutting it. Cut into strips about 3 1/2 inches long and about 1/4-inch wide. Mix together the cayenne pepper, salt, and garlic powder; equally season the steak with this seasoning mixture. Let it stand for a few minutes.

In a large skillet over high heat, add the peanut oil and heat until it starts to smoke. Add the meat, shallots, garlic, and ginger. Sauté until the meat is well browned. Remove from the pan onto a warm platter.

Add the celery, green pepper, red pepper, and onions and sauté for 3 minutes.

Add the meat-ginger mixture back to the skillet. Put the water chestnuts in the skillet and blend them in. Pour on the soy sauce, beef stock, red wine, and Worcestershire sauce and reduce the heat to simmer. Stir until well blended. Add the sugar and Tabasco sauce. Mix together the cornstarch and cold water, then add to the pan with the green onions and parsley. Blend in well. The sauce will thicken as it is heated. When thickened, serve hot over cooked white rice. Serves 8.

Lagniappe: You can make this recipe in advance and store in the refrigerator, but you lose the crispness of the vegetables. The flavor will not be lessened. Do not freeze. This is an easy recipe and the bulk of the time is spent in preparation for cooking. If you do all your cutting and chopping beforehand, the time is not long. This recipe can easily be made in a wok.

Calories — 422; Carb — 14.5; Fat — 22.3; Chol — 92.0; Pro — 39.2; Fib — 1.0

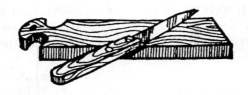

BEEFSTEAK CANTRELLE

4 (3 1/2 oz. each) beef cube
  steaks
vegetable oil spray, butter
  flavor
1 tbsp. butter, unsalted (or
  margarine)
1/2 tsp. salt
1/2 tsp. white pepper
1/4 tsp. red pepper
1/2 tsp. onion powder
1 clove garlic, minced
1 tbsp. celery

1/2 cup green onions,
  chopped
8 large mushrooms, sliced
1/4 cup hearty burgundy
  wine
1/4 tsp. sweet basil
1/8 tsp. rosemary
1/2 tsp. salt
1/4 tsp. Tabasco sauce
3 tbsp. half-and-half
  cream

Spread the 4 steaks out with the palm of your hand. Heat the skillet over medium-high heat until it is hot, then remove from the heat and spray with the vegetable oil spray. Add the butter and return to the heat. When the butter starts to smoke, add the steaks and cook them 2 minutes on each side; remove from the skillet and place them on a warm serving plate. Season with the salt, white pepper, red pepper, and onion powder. Set them aside for later use.

Reduce the heat to medium, then add the garlic, green onions, celery, and mushrooms to the skillet and sauté them for 3 minutes, stirring constantly. Add the wine and deglaze the pan by stirring until the brown spots on the pan surface have dissolved. Add the remaining ingredients and blend in well. Bring the sauce to a simmer, but do not let it boil. It will thicken somewhat. Spoon an equal amount of sautéed vegetables and sauce on top of each steak. Serve at once. Serves 4.

Lagniappe: This dish cannot be made in advance. The meat will lose its taste and tenderness. This is really just plain cube steak, but it is garnished so nicely that it is lifted from the ordinary to the sublime. Total cooking time is only about 10 minutes, so you don't need a lot of time to cook.

Calories — 326; Carb — 2.7; Fat — 18.0; Chol — 93.3; Pro — 32.1; Fib — 0.6

PORK TENDERLOIN MICHELLE

1 lb. pork tenderloin
vegetable oil spray, butter
 flavor
1 tsp. sesame oil
1/2 tsp. salt
1/2 tsp. cayenne pepper
1/4 tsp. white pepper
1/2 tsp. garlic powder
1/2 tsp. fresh oregano
 or 1/4 tsp. dry leaves
1 clove garlic, minced
1 tbsp. carrot, minced
1 tbsp. celery, minced
1/4 cup A-1 steak sauce
2 tbsp. reduced calorie
 catsup
1/2 cup green onions,
 chopped
1/2 cup beef stock or beef
 broth
1 tbsp. Worcestershire
 sauce
1 tbsp. soy sauce
1 tbsp. fresh lemon juice
2 tbsp. hearty burgundy
 wine
1 tbsp. cornstarch
1/8 tsp. Tabasco sauce
2 cups cooked white rice
 or egg noodles
2 tbsp. fresh parsley,
 minced

Trim the tenderloin of any fat and slice it into thin slices (less than 1/4-inch thick). Heat a heavy nonstick skillet over medium-high heat until hot. Remove from the heat and spray with the vegetable oil spray. Add the sesame oil and fry the pieces of pork on one side for 1 minute. Season with the salt, cayenne pepper, white pepper, garlic powder, and oregano, then turn over and add the garlic, carrot, and celery; fry for 1 more minute. Add the A-1 steak sauce, reduce the heat to medium, and braise the tenderloin for 2 minutes, stirring often. Add the catsup and green onions and cook for 2 more minutes, stirring. Add the beef stock and simmer for 3 minutes.

Mix together the remaining ingredients, except for the last two, until the cornstarch dissolves. Pour into the hot skillet and let the sauce simmer until it thickens. Serve over 1/2 cup of cooked white rice or 1/2 cup of cooked egg noodles per serving. Garnish with the parsley and serve at once. Serves 4.

Lagniappe: This dish should be eaten right after it is made. You can prepare all your ingredients in advance. Cooking time is just about

12 minutes. You can refrigerate leftovers (if there are any), but the quality of the dish will be lower. Just simmer over low heat until warm and serve.

Calories — 443; Carb — 34.0; Fat — 12.0; Chol — 80.0; Pro — 38.3; Fib — 0.6

VEAL SCALLOPINI AGUILLARD

**4 scallopini of veal, about
  3 1/2 oz. each
1/2 tbsp. all-purpose flour
1/2 tbsp. whole wheat
  flour
1/4 tsp. salt
1/4 tsp. red pepper
1/4 tsp. garlic powder
vegetable oil spray, butter
  flavor
1 1/2 tbsp. butter,
  unsalted (or margarine)**

**2 tbsp. extra dry vermouth
1/4 cup chicken stock or
  chicken broth
2 tbsp. tomato paste
1/4 cup sweet red
  bell pepper
1/4 cup ripe black olives,
  sliced
2 tbsp. green onions,
  chopped
1 tbsp. fresh parsley**

Inspect the scallopini to make sure that there is no excess fat or hard muscle. Mix together the two flours until blended and add the salt, red pepper, and garlic powder. Mix together well. Spray a heavy skillet with the vegetable oil spray and place over medium heat until hot. Add the butter and let it melt.

As the butter is melting, and not before, lightly coat the scallopini with the seasoned flour. The butter should be smoking when you finish; quickly add the flour-coated scallopini to the skillet. Fry for 1 1/2 minutes on the first side, then turn the veal over and fry for 2 1/2 minutes. Turn the veal over and fry 1 1/2 more minutes on the first side. Don't try to save work and fry for 3 minutes on the first side before you turn; it will make the flour pick up too much moisture on the second side and you will lose the light crispness on that side. Remove to a warm platter and add the vermouth to the pan. Stir around and shake the pan, then add the chicken stock. Deglaze the pan by dissolving the dark particles into the liquid. Add the remaining ingredients and cook for 2 minutes, stirring constantly. Place 1 veal scallopini on each of four serving plates and sauce with the skillet contents. Serve at once. Serves 4.

Lagniappe: Don't let the length of the recipe fool you; this is very easy. Total cooking time is under 8 minutes. Read through once and you'll see that this is very simple. When I write simple recipes, I try to make sure that I leave nothing to chance (I hope I'm not rationalizing). Just follow through as above and you'll succeed. Let me emphasize one thing: do not dredge the veal in the flour in advance of the cooking. It will make the flour dusting turn to a heavy batter if you do. Do not make in advance and, of course, you can't freeze this dish.

Calories — 397; Carb — 4.4; Fat — 22.9; Chol — 102.6; Pro — 34.4; Fib — 0.5

VEAL CHOW MEIN

vegetable oil spray
1 1/2 lb. ground veal
1 clove garlic, minced
1 medium yellow onion,
chopped
1/2 cup bell peppers,
chopped
1 cup cauliflower florets,
steamed for 2 minutes
2 cups baby carrots, whole
and steamed for
2 minutes

1/2 cup green onions, cut
1 inch long
1 can (6 oz.) water
chestnuts, sliced
1 cup beef stock or beef
broth
2 tbsp. cornstarch
2 tsp. sugar
1/4 tsp. Tabasco sauce
2 tbsp. soy sauce
chow mein noodles or
cooked white rice

Heat a large skillet over medium heat until hot. Spray with vegetable oil spray, then add the veal, garlic, and onions. Sauté until the meat is browned. Add the bell pepper and sauté 1 more minute. Add the florets, carrots, green onions, and water chestnuts; sauté for 2 minutes.

Mix together the beef stock, cornstarch, sugar, Tabasco, and soy sauce until the cornstarch has completely dissolved. Pour over the veal-vegetable mixture and bring to a boil; the minute it begins to boil, reduce the heat to a low simmer and cover. Cook for 5 minutes. Serve hot over chow mein noodles or cooked white rice or both. Serves 6.

Lagniappe: This dish can be made in advance, but is better if eaten right away. Just refrigerate until ready to use and heat in the microwave or on stovetop over low heat until heated through.

You can substitute 1 1/2 pounds chicken cut into bite-size pieces for the veal to make **Chicken Chow Mein,** making sure to change the beef stock to chicken stock. You can substitute 1 1/2 pounds of ground round to make **Beef Chow Mein.** This is, then, three recipes in one. Also feel free to substitute other vegetables for the carrots and cauliflower; just keep the proportions equal. A real feast!

VEAL: Calories — 388; Carb — 15.0; Fat — 17.5; Chol — 103.0; Pro — 40.1; Fib — 1.1

CHICKEN: Calories — 260; Carb — 16.0; Fat — 6.7; Chol — 97.0; Pro — 37.7; Fib — 1.1

BEEF: Calories — 366; Carb — 15.0; Fat — 17.9; Chol — 140.0; Pro — 38.9; Fib — 1.1

BEEF MEDALLIONS CALHOUN

4 2-oz. each beef medal-
   lions (tenderloin of beef)
1 1/2 tbsp. all-purpose
   flour
1/4 tsp. cayenne pepper
1/4 tsp. garlic powder
1/8 tsp. white pepper
2 tbsp. butter, unsalted
3/4 tsp. salt
1/4 tsp. sweet basil
2 oz. lean ham, julienned

1 clove garlic, minced
1/2 tsp. shallots, minced
1 cup beef stock or beef
   broth
1/4 cup dry hearty
   burgundy wine
1 medium lemon, juice
   only
1/4 tsp. Tabasco sauce
cooked noodles, white
   rice, or potatoes

Take the medallions of beef, put them between two pieces of plastic wrap, and pound them with a mallet until they increase one-third in size. Mix together well the flour, cayenne pepper, garlic powder, and white pepper. Dust equally each of the medallions.

In a skillet over high heat, add the butter and as soon as it starts to smoke, sauté the medallions for 1 minute on each side. Remove the medallions to a warm plate, season with the salt and sweet basil, and keep the medallions warm while continuing with the recipe.

Add the julienned ham, garlic, and shallots to the skillet, reduce the heat to medium, and sauté for 2 minutes. Deglaze the pan with the stock, burgundy wine, lemon juice, and Tabasco, taking care to stir and scrape the bottom of the pan to get all the pan drippings into solution. Raise the heat to high and reduce the liquid by one-third. Add the medallions back to the skillet, reduce the heat to simmer, and let the medallions simmer for 4 minutes. Serve hot over cooked noodles, white rice, or potatoes, making sure the sauce is over the meat and noodles. Serves 2.

Lagniappe: Do not make this dish in advance. It is quick, so there is no
   need to do so. You can pound the meat in advance, to save some

time, but do not dust the meat with the flour until you are ready to cook. It will become soggy and you will lose texture and quality. If you want to make a richer sauce, you can add 1/2 cup of heavy cream after the liquid has been reduced by the one-third. Then follow the recipe as above.

Calories — 371; Carb — 9.7; Fat — 26.1; Chol — 103.5; Pro — 44.9; Fib — 0.3

SZECHUAN BEEF

1 1/2 tbsp. peanut oil
1 lb. flank steak, thinly sliced
3 cloves garlic, minced
2 tsp. shallots, minced
1/4 lb. snow pea pods, washed and stem removed
1 cup broccoli florets
1/2 cup bell pepper, coarsely chopped
6 large mushrooms, sliced
1/2 cup celery, cut into 1/2-inch diagonal pieces
1/2 cup bok choy, chopped
1 can (6 oz.) water chestnuts, sliced

1 tsp. salt
2 tsp. sugar
1/4 tsp. Tabasco sauce
1/4 tsp. sweet basil
1/4 tsp. fresh grated ginger
1/2 tsp. dry hot mustard
1/2 cup cold water
1 tbsp. cornstarch
2 tbsp. soy sauce
1/2 tsp. crushed red pepper flakes
1 tsp. toasted sesame seeds
3 cups cooked white rice
paprika for garnish

Heat a large skillet over high heat until hot. Add the oil and heat until it smokes, then quickly add the flank steak, garlic, and shallots; sauté quickly just until the meat is browned but still has a little pink showing. Move to the side of the skillet. Add the vegetables and water chestnuts; toss them in well to get the oil to coat them as much as possible.

Reduce the heat to medium, cover, and cook for 3 minutes, shaking the pan a few times while the vegetables are cooking. Add the seasonings through the dry mustard and stir in well. Mix together the cold water and cornstarch until dissolved and pour into the skillet. Stir through. Add the remaining ingredients except for the rice and paprika and stir through until the sauce thickens. Serve at once over the cooked white rice and sprinkle with paprika. Serves 6.

Lagniappe: Do not do anything in advance but prepare the meat and vegetables. This is a quick-cooking one-dish meal. A nice dry red wine and a crisp salad will do well with your entree. Read through the recipe before you start. Don't let the list of ingredients throw you; it really is quite easy.

Calories — 380; Carb — 38.1; Fat — 4.6; Chol — 140.0; Pro — 31.1; Fib — 1.2

BEEF ROSEMARY

2 tbsp. butter, unsalted
1 tsp. rosemary, crumbled
1/8 tsp. thyme
1 clove garlic, minced
1 1/2 tbsp. all-purpose
   flour
1/4 tsp. red pepper
1/4 tsp. white pepper
1/4 tsp. onion powder
4 (6 oz. each) beef
   tenderloin fillets

8 large mushrooms, sliced
1/4 cup onions, minced
1/2 tsp. dry mustard
1 tsp. Worcestershire
   sauce
1/4 tsp. Tabasco sauce
1 tsp. salt
1/4 cup brandy
1/4 cup beef stock or beef
   broth
2 tbsp. fresh parsley,
   minced

In a skillet over medium-high heat, melt the butter with the rosemary, thyme, and garlic. Mix together the flour, red pepper, white pepper, and onion powder and lightly dust the fillets with the flour mixture. When the butter is hot and begins to smoke, sauté the fillets in the seasoned butter to brown both sides, about 1 minute on each side. Add the mushrooms, onions, dry mustard, Worcestershire sauce, and Tabasco and continue to sauté until beef is cooked to the doneness that you like (about 4 minutes for medium).

When the meat is done, remove the skillet from the heat. Add the salt, taking care to salt each fillet equally, add the brandy, and stir throughout. Take care when adding the brandy; it can catch fire as the alcohol heats. As soon as the bubbles die down, add the beef stock and fresh parsley. Allow the sauce to thicken slightly. Remove the fillets to warm serving plates and pour the sauce over them. Serve at once. Serves 4.

Lagniappe: All you can do in advance is get your ingredients lined up. This is a quick recipe and you should be able to do it with little effort.

You can substitute veal medallions for the beef fillets and make **Veal Rosemary.** All you do is substitute two 2-ounce veal medallions for each beef fillet. Also, you would cut the 4 minute cooking time down to 1 minute. Either recipe is quick and tasty.

Calories — 499; Carb — 5.4; Fat — 21.8; Chol — 154.5; Pro — 54.3; Fib — 0.4

VEAL CUBE STEAK IDELL

1 lb. veal cube steak, 4
steaks (4 oz. each)
vegetable oil spray, butter
flavor
1 tbsp. butter, unsalted (or
margarine)
salt and black pepper to
taste
1/2 tsp. onion powder
1/4 tsp. garlic powder
1/4 tsp. sweet basil

1 tsp. shallots, minced
1 cup oyster mushrooms,
whole
1/4 cup brandy
3 tbsp. sour cream
1 tsp. Worcestershire
sauce
1/8 tsp. Tabasco sauce
2 tbsp. fresh parsley,
minced

Trim any excess fat from the veal cube steaks. Spray a large, heavy skillet with the vegetable oil spray and add the butter. Heat over medium-high heat until the butter melts and begins to smoke. Add the cube steaks and sauté for 2 minutes. Turn over and season to taste with salt and black pepper. Season equally with the onion powder, garlic powder, and sweet basil, then add the shallots and oyster mushrooms. Cook the steak for 2 1/2 minutes on the second side, then add the brandy. Let it heat for a second, then flambé, taking care not to blow the kitchen! There will be a puff and a very hot fire. Be ready when the match is put to it. Simply shake the pan, gently, until the fire dies out on its own. Add the remaining ingredients and blend them in well. Arrange the steaks on four individual warm serving plates and garnish them with the sauce and mushrooms. Serve at once. Serves 4.

Lagniappe: Well, this is another recipe that can't be made in advance. But look at the time! You can do this in about 6 minutes. Now really! Do you need to do anything in advance? It's easy and it tastes great. You'll wonder why you ever ate so poorly before and with all those calories that you used to take in.

Calories—422; Carb—4.6; Fat—22.6; Chol—114.3; Pro—39.3; Fib—0.3

Poultry

Poultry is an excellent source of protein. This is the meat to choose if you are looking for low calories, fat, and cholesterol. Chicken and turkey are easy to cook and allow a larger meat portion than red meats. The white meat is lower in fat content and therefore lower in calories. Be sure to remove the skin from the poultry before cooking; this helps keep the calories and fat down. Never buy self-basted poultry, since it means fat has been added, usually a saturated fat or sometimes butter. This costs more and adds a great deal of calories, fat, and cholesterol to the meat.

The recipes in this section are simple, and you will find the calorie count most acceptable. Serving size is generous. Chicken and turkey are excellent buys as well. You get a good deal of protein for your money.

Be sure to cook according to directions. Often poultry is either undercooked or overcooked. Both are serious problems. It will not affect your health, but taste, texture, and appearance are severely damaged by either.

Be sure to read the lagniappe section under each recipe. There are plenty of suggestions that will be helpful and many ideas for changing the recipe to create new dishes.

CHICKEN ASHLEY

vegetable oil spray
2 cups baked chicken
   breast, cut into bite-size
   cubes
1 large onion, cut into
   chunks
3 tbsp. soy sauce
1/4 cup pineapple juice,
   unsweetened
1 tbsp. Worcestershire
   sauce
1/4 tsp. Tabasco sauce

1 package (10 oz.)
   asparagus spears,
   defrosted and sliced
4 large mushrooms, thinly
   sliced
1/4 cup cream sherry
1 tbsp. cornstarch
1/2 cup seedless green
   grapes, cut in half
1/2 cup cherry tomatoes,
   cut in half

Use the vegetable oil spray to coat a large, heavy nonstick skillet and place the skillet over medium heat. Add the chicken, onions, and soy sauce to the skillet. Cook covered for 2 minutes. Add the juice, Worcestershire sauce, and Tabasco and cook covered for 5 to 7 minutes. Add the asparagus and mushrooms; cook for 5 more minutes. Blend the sherry with the cornstarch and mix into the skillet. Cook, stirring constantly, until the sauce thickens. Add the grapes and cherry tomatoes and simmer for 1 more minute. Serve hot. Serves 4.

Lagniappe: This has to be made just before you are ready to eat, but you can do the chopping in advance. Total cooking time is under 15 minutes. You can serve over rice if you like or just eat as is.
   You can use this same recipe with leftover turkey breast by substituting 2 cups of cubed cooked turkey breast for the chicken to make **Turkey Breast Ashley.**

Calories — 195; Carb — 22.3; Fat — 2.2; Chol — 36.5; Pro — 18.5; Fib — 1.5

ING FUN CHICKEN

frozen

ves

1 tsp. salt
1/2 tsp. onion powder
1/2 tsp. garlic powder
1/4 tsp. sweet basil
1/4 tsp. dry hot mustard
2 medium white onions,
   sliced 1/4-inch thick and
   separated into rings

1 cup sweet red bell
   pepper, julienned
2 tbsp. celery, minced
2 cloves garlic, minced
2 tbsp. olive oil
2 tbsp. butter or margarine
1/3 cup brandy
1/4 cup green onions,
   chopped
3 cups cooked white rice
2 tbsp. fresh parsley,
   chopped

Take the chicken breasts, place them between a layer of plastic wrap, and pound them with a kitchen mallet until they increase in size by one-third. Cut the chicken into strips about 1/4-inch thick and about 2 1/2 inches long. Mix together all the dry spices until well blended. Season the chicken strips well with the spice mixture and place in a deep container that has a tight-fitting cover. Place about one-third of the chicken on the bottom, and cover it with one-third of the onions, red pepper, celery, and garlic. Sprinkle a little of the spice mixture that remains on top of the vegetables. Repeat the process until all the chicken and vegetables are used. Tightly cover and let the chicken sit in the refrigerator overnight or at least 8 hours.

When you are ready to cook, heat a large, heavy skillet over medium-high heat until it is hot. Add the olive oil and butter; let the butter melt. When the butter starts to smoke, add the chicken to the skillet and cover with the onions, red peppers, celery, and garlic. Cook at medium-high heat until the chicken is browned on all sides, about 5 to 7 minutes.

Reduce the temperature to low and carefully add the brandy. Strike a match and bring it carefully to the skillet; there will be a puff and a hot fire. BE CAREFUL! If you are not used to working with a flambé, you may want to watch someone cook this first. Do not shake the pan or stir; the flame will go out naturally. When it does, stir the chicken well. Add the green onions and cook for 1 minute. Add the rice and parsley; mix together well and serve at once. Serves 6.

Lagniappe: Do not freeze. You cannot refrigerate this dish after it is cooked without losing quality, but you can refrigerate the seasoned chicken before cooking for up to 3 days. It will actually improve the flavor; the seasonings will be able to merge together well. Cooking time is very short and this is truly a dish you will want to prepare in front of your family or guests. Please do be cautious with the flambé. Serve with a nice green vegetable. This is a simple dish, but it is quite showy and the taste is absolutely fabulous.

Calories — 383; Carb — 28.1; Fat — 12.4; Chol — 91.8; Pro — 32.8; Fib — 0.9

SWEET AND SOUR CHICKEN

1 lb. chicken breast,
  skinned and boned
1 tbsp. peanut oil
1 cup chicken stock or
  chicken broth
1 medium green pepper,
  julienned
1/2 cup celery, chopped
1 medium onion, sliced
1 tbsp. cornstarch
3 tbsp. soy sauce

1 can (17 oz.) pineapple
  chunks, unsweetened
  with juice
1 tsp. Worcestershire
  sauce
1 1/2 tbsp. red wine
  vinegar
1/4 tsp. Tabasco sauce
1 drop red food coloring
2 cups cooked white or
  brown rice

In a large, heavy nonstick skillet over medium-high heat, add the oil and heat until it begins to smoke. Cut the chicken into bite-size strips. When the oil is smoking, add the chicken and quickly fry until the chicken is nicely browned on all sides.

Wipe the pan lightly with a paper towel to remove any remaining grease. Add the chicken stock, green pepper, celery, and onions and bring the liquid to a boil, then reduce immediately to a simmer. Separate the liquid from the pineapple chunks and add the pineapple juice to the chicken stock mixture. Cover and continue to simmer for 30 minutes or until the chicken is very tender. Add the pineapple chunks and stir in well.

Mix together the cornstarch, soy sauce, Worcestershire sauce, vinegar, and Tabasco sauce until the cornstarch is dissolved. Pour the cornstarch mixture into the simmering liquid. Blend in well. The sauce will begin to thicken nicely. Add the drop of food coloring to the sauce and blend in until the color is uniform. Serve hot over or on the side of cooked white or brown rice. Serves 4.

Lagniappe: It is possible to make this dish ahead of time and refrigerate for later use. Do not freeze. Just return to the heat over simmer until hot. I like to eat this dish right after cooking. It loses some of its zest when you refrigerate. Sometimes we must refrigerate! If you are in one of those situations, this recipe will do nicely for you. You can use this recipe to make great **Sweet and Sour Turkey.** Just substitute 1 pound of fresh turkey breast and cut into slices. Make exactly as above. This recipe will also work to make a great **Sweet and Sour Pork,** by using 1 pound of pork tenderloin instead of the chicken.

Calories — 403; Carb — 51.2; Fat — 4.1; Chol — 98.0; Pro — 41.2; Fib — 1.2

RITZY CHICKEN

1 cup Ritz cracker crumbs
1/4 cup Romano cheese,
    grated
2 tbsp. Parmesan cheese,
    grated
3 tbsp. fresh parsley,
    minced
1 tbsp. green onion tops,
    minced
1 tsp. salt

1/4 tsp.
1/8 tsp.
1/4 tsp
1/4 tsp
2 whol
    chic____
    skinned and boned
2 tbsp. diet margarine,
    melted

Preheat the oven to 350 degrees. Mix together well the Ritz crackers, cheeses, and spices. Cut the chicken breasts in half, then use a kitchen mallet to tenderize the breast and break up some of the fibers. Dip, lightly, each piece of chicken in the margarine and roll in the Ritz-seasoning mixture. Place in a baking dish and drizzle the remaining melted margarine on the chicken. Bake for 1 hour. Do not turn; it will make the chicken soggy. Serve at once. Serves 4.

Lagniappe: Do not cook and refrigerate, but you can prepare up to the baking point and refrigerate until you are ready to cook. This crunchy chicken is easy and tasty. You can use this same crumb mixture to oven-fry pork chops.

Calories — 475; Carb — 12.5; Fat — 19.4; Chol — 162.0; Pro — 60.6; Fib — 0.3

BREAST OF CHICKEN
NICOLE MARIE

whole (12 oz. each)
chicken breasts,
skinned, boned and cut
in half
1/2 tsp. red pepper
1 tsp. salt
1/4 tsp. black pepper
1 tbsp. all-purpose flour
1/4 cup peanut oil
2 cloves garlic, minced
1 tsp. sweet basil
1 tsp. rosemary
1/2 tsp. thyme
1 large green bell pepper,
cut into strips

1 large red bell pepper, cut
into strips
1 small purple onion, cut
into slices
2 tbsp. fresh parsley,
minced
1/2 cup dry vermouth
1/4 tsp. Tabasco sauce
1 tbsp. white
Worcestershire sauce
1/4 cup stewed tomatoes
1/4 cup green onions,
chopped

Take each cut chicken breast and pound it a few times with a kitchen mallet, just to be sure the fibers are tender. Season with red pepper, salt, and black pepper. Dust with the flour lightly and evenly. In a large skillet over medium-high heat, add the peanut oil and heat it until it begins to smoke. Carefully place each breast half in the hot oil and sauté each side until it is golden brown, about 2 minutes on each side. Remove the chicken to a warm platter for a few minutes.

Add the garlic, sweet basil, rosemary, and thyme; sauté for 1 minute. Add the green bell pepper, red bell pepper, and purple onion and sauté for 2 minutes over medium-high heat. Add the parsley and stir it through, then add the chicken breasts back into the skillet. Reduce the heat to medium and add the dry vermouth, Tabasco sauce, and white Worcestershire sauce. Shake the skillet and allow the wine sauce to reduce almost completely. Add the stewed tomatoes and green onions and cook for 2 more minutes, constantly shaking the pan and spooning the vegetables and sauce over the chicken breasts. Serve hot with plenty of peppers and sauce over each breast. Serves 4.

Lagniappe: Since this dish cooks so quickly there is no need to refrigerate for later use. It does not freeze well. You can chop all the ingredients in advance to save a little time, but please serve right after cooking.

You can also make **Veal Nicole Marie,** using the same recipe, except use veal medallions (about 3 ounces each) instead of the chicken breasts. Cook the veal for 1 minute per side, then follow the recipe above. The dish is excellent with either chicken or veal. This is a really nice company dish that is quick but tasty.

Calories — 398; Carb — 7.4; Fat — 10.1; Chol — 145.5; Pro — 55.2; Fib — 1.3

HONEY-PORT BRAISED
TURKEY BREAST

1 lb. turkey breast tenderloin
vegetable oil spray, butter
  flavor
2 tbsp. peanut oil
6 medium green onions,
  chopped
1 tbsp. fresh ginger,
  minced

2 cloves garlic, minced
3 tbsp. honey
1/4 cup port wine
2 tbsp. tamari soy sauce
1 tsp. red wine vinegar
1/4 cup chicken stock or
  chicken broth
2 tbsp. fresh parsley,
  minced

Slice the turkey tenderloins in slices that are about 1/2-inch thick. Spray a heavy skillet with the vegetable oil spray and heat the skillet over medium-high heat. Add the peanut oil and let it get hot. When it starts to smoke, add the green onions, ginger, and garlic. Sauté for 1 minute, then add the slices of turkey tenderloin. Brown quickly on both sides. While the turkey is browning, mix together the honey, port wine, and soy sauce and set aside for later use.

Once the turkey is well browned, add the vinegar and stir in. Add the chicken stock and let it mix with the pan juices. Cook for 1 minute, stirring constantly. Pour the honey-wine mixture into the skillet, cover, and reduce the heat to a low simmer. Simmer covered for 20 minutes, then garnish with fresh parsley. Serve at once. Serves 4.

Lagniappe: This is a quick dish, but you can save some time by making the recipe up to the simmering point. Remove and let the pan cool, then refrigerate. When you are ready to serve, just cover the pot, put it at simmer, and simmer for 20 minutes; garnish with fresh parsley.

Calories — 353; Carb — 18.1; Fat — 12.8; Chol — 87.0; Pro — 19.3; Fib — 0.5

ORANGE CHICKEN

**2 whole (10 oz. each)
chicken breasts, cut in
half**
**1 1/2 tsp. finely grated
orange peel**
1/4 tsp. garlic, minced
**1 tbsp. green onions,
minced**
1/4 tsp. ginger
1/4 tsp. Tabasco sauce

**1/4 tsp. fresh ground black
pepper**
1/4 tsp. arrowroot
**1 1/2 tbsp. fresh orange
juice**
3 tbsp. honey
2 tsp. soy sauce
1 tbsp. dry white wine
1/2 tsp. salt

Preheat the oven to broil. Take each chicken breast half, place it on a cutting board, and pound with a meat mallet until about 1/2-inch thick. Set the breasts aside for later use. In a mixing bowl, add all the remaining ingredients and mix together well. Put the chicken breasts on a broiler pan rack and, with a pastry brush, brush them generously with the orange-honey sauce. Place them under the broiler about 4 inches from the heat and broil for 7 to 8 minutes or until tender. Baste with the sauce every 2 minutes during the broiling. Serve at once. Serves 4.

Lagniappe: This is an excellent, quick, low-calorie dish. You can mix your sauce and pound your chicken breasts in advance, so the cooking time of 7 or 8 minutes is the only time necessary to get the meal to the table.

Calories — 195; Carb — 14.0; Fat — 3.0; Chol — 72.0; Pro — 27.0; Fib — 0.1

QUICK CHICKEN SKILLET

1 1/2 tbsp. Worcestershire sauce
3 tbsp. Chenin Blanc wine, or dry white wine
1 1/2 tbsp. soy sauce
2 tbsp. fresh lemon juice
1/4 tbsp. Tabasco sauce
1 tbsp. cornstarch
1 1/2 lb. chicken breasts, skinned and boned
1 cup carrots, julienned
1 cup broccoli florets
1/2 cup celery, julienned
1/2 cup green pepper, julienned
1 cup sweet red bell pepper, julienned
6 large mushrooms, sliced
water for steamer
2 tbsp. peanut oil
2 tbsp. butter, unsalted or margarine
2 cloves garlic, minced
2 tsp. shallots, minced
2 tsp. sugar
1/4 tsp. sweet basil
1/2 tsp. dry hot mustard
1/2 tsp. fresh lemon peel, yellow only
1 tsp. fresh grated ginger
1/4 cup fresh parsley, minced
cooked white rice

In a large mixing bowl, combine the Worcestershire sauce, wine, soy sauce, lemon juice, Tabasco, and cornstarch and blend together until cornstarch is dissolved. Place the chicken breasts between some plastic wrap and pound with a kitchen mallet until the size is increased by about one-fourth, then cut into bite-size strips. Add them to the bowl and coat them well. Let the chicken marinate in the liquid for 20 minutes.

Add the carrots, broccoli, celery, green pepper, mushrooms, and red pepper to a steamer and place a little water in the bottom. Bring to a full boil and when the steam begins to rise strongly, time 2 minutes. Remove from the fire and let the vegetables stand in the steamer for 5 minutes. Remove, drain, and set aside for later use.

When the chicken has finished marinating, heat a large skillet over medium-high heat until the pan is hot. Add the peanut oil and let it get hot, then add the butter. When the butter melts and the oil begins to smoke, add the chicken, garlic, and shallots, taking care not to get splashed with the oil. Sauté quickly, about 5 to 7 minutes, or until the chicken is nicely browned and the meat is white and puffy. Add the vegetables, pour in what is remaining of the marinade, add the remaining ingredients except for the rice, and mix together well. Serve at once over the cooked white rice. Serves 6.

Lagniappe: This dish cannot be refrigerated or frozen. You can do all the preparations in advance, like steaming the vegetables and marinating the chicken, so all that will be left is the quick cooking process. You can let the chicken breasts marinate overnight if you like. It is possible to use the dark meat from the chicken instead of the chicken breast, if you desire.

Calories — 320; Carb — 10.7; Fat — 12.9; Chol — 97.0; Pro — 38.1; Fib — 1.1

TENDERLOIN OF TURKEY CRYSTAL

1 lb. turkey tenderloin
vegetable oil spray, butter flavor
2 tbsp. diet margarine
1/2 tsp. salt
1/2 tsp. onion powder
1/4 tsp. red pepper
1/4 tsp. sweet basil
1 1/2 tsp. shallots, minced

2 tbsp. canned green peppercorns, drained
8 large mushrooms, thinly sliced
1/2 cup extra dry vermouth
2 tsp. Butter Buds
1 tbsp. green onion tops, minced

Cut the tenderloins of turkey into slices about 3/8-inch thick. Spray a heavy skillet with the vegetable spray and place on medium-high heat. When the skillet is hot, add the margarine. When the margarine starts to smoke, fry the tenderloin slices for 3 minutes on the first side. Turn the slices over and sauté for 3 more minutes, constantly shaking the pan to prevent sticking. Remove the turkey to a warm holding platter for later use and season it with the salt, onion powder, red pepper, and sweet basil.

Put the shallots and green peppercorns into the skillet and sauté for 2 minutes. Add the mushrooms and sauté them for 2 more minutes. Add the vermouth and deglaze the pan by getting the brown particles on the pan's bottom to dissolve in the liquid. The sauce should thicken somewhat. Add the Butter Buds and blend in well. Return the turkey to the skillet and simmer for 2 minutes. Stir in the green onion tops and serve at once. Be sure to serve plenty of mushrooms on top of the turkey slices. Serves 4.

Lagniappe: This is better if eaten right after it is cooked. The fresh mushrooms lose some of their body and fresh flavor if you refrigerate. Cooking time is low, so just assemble all the ingredients in advance and you'll get through this with ease.

Calories — 258; Carb — 4.9; Fat — 9.1; Chol — 86.8; Pro — 18.6; Fib — 0.5

SAUTE OF
TURKEY PISIQUIT

4 4-oz. turkey cutlets
vegetable oil spray, butter
   flavor
1 tbsp. butter, unsalted or
   margarine
1 tsp. olive oil, extra virgin
1 tsp. salt
1/2 tsp. black pepper
1/2 tsp. white pepper
1/2 tsp. fresh sage,
   chopped (or 1/8 tsp. dry)

1/4 tsp. garlic powder
2 cloves garlic, minced
1 cup Shiitake
   mushrooms, whole
1 tbsp. capers
1/4 cup brandy
1/4 cup evaporated milk
1 tbsp. fresh lemon juice
1 tsp. white Worces-
   tershire sauce
1/8 tsp. Tabasco sauce

1/4 tsp. fresh rosemary (or 1/8 tsp. dried crushed leaves)	2 tbsp. fresh parsley, minced
1/2 tsp. onion powder	1 tbsp. green onions, minced

Take the turkey cutlets and place them between two pieces of plastic wrap. Pound them about 4 times each with a kitchen mallet. Spray a large, heavy skillet with the vegetable oil spray, then add the butter and olive oil. Heat over medium heat until the butter melts and begins to smoke. Add the turkey and sauté for 3 minutes on each side.

While the turkey is cooking, mix together well the salt, black pepper, white pepper, sage, rosemary, onion powder, and garlic powder. When the turkey has cooked for the 6 minutes, sprinkle equally with the seasoned mixture. Add the garlic, mushrooms, and capers; blend everything together well, reduce the heat, and simmer for 2 minutes. Add the brandy and let it heat for a second, then put a match to it and let it flambé. Take care! There will be a pop and a very hot fire. Simply shake the pan, gently, until the fire dies out on its own. Add all but the last two remaining ingredients and blend them in well. Let the sauce simmer for 2 or 3 minutes; it should begin to thicken nicely. Arrange the cutlets on four individual warm serving plates and garnish them with the sauce and mushrooms. Serve at once. Serves 4.

Lagniappe: This is another recipe that can't be made in advance but it only takes about 10 minutes. You'll wonder how something so zesty can be so low-calorie. Tasting this recipe will have you talking turkey from now on!

Calories — 332; Carb — 6.6; Fat — 14.1; Chol — 96.3; Pro — 13.3; Fib — 0.4

PECAN CHICKEN

2 whole (12 oz. each),
large chicken breasts,
skinned, boned and cut
in half
2 1/2 tsp. cornstarch
3 tbsp. soy sauce
3 tbsp. dry sherry
1 tbsp. fresh lemon juice
1 tsp sugar
1/2 tsp. salt
1/4 tsp. Tabasco sauce
1 tsp. fresh grated ginger

1/4 tsp. crushed red
pepper flakes
2 tbsp. peanut oil
2 large bell peppers,
coarsely chopped
1 small onion, cut into
quarters
1 cup green onions, cut
into 1-inch pieces
1/2 cup pecan halves,
broken into large pieces
cooked white rice

Cut the chicken into bite-size pieces and set aside for later use. Mix together well the cornstarch, soy sauce, sherry, lemon juice, sugar, salt, Tabasco, red pepper flakes, and ginger, then set aside for later use. Heat a large skillet over high heat until it is hot, then add the peanut oil.

When the oil is hot, sauté the bell peppers, onion, and green onions for 2 minutes. Remove from the skillet. Add the pecans and sauté for 2 minutes, then remove from the pan, taking care to leave all the oil possible behind.

Sauté one-half of the chicken for 2 minutes, remove the first batch from the pan, then sauté the remaining chicken for 2 minutes. Return all the chicken to the skillet and stir in the cornstarch-soy sauce mixture, making sure to blend together completely. The sauce should thicken and bubble. Stir in the sautéed vegetables and pecans; cover and cook for an additional minute. Serve at once over the cooked white rice. Serves 6.

Lagniappe: Plan on eating immediately after cooking if you want this dish at its best. You can refrigerate leftovers for later use, but you will lose a lot of the taste, appearance, and texture of the dish after refrigerating. Reheat in the microwave or on stovetop over low heat. By substituting bite-size pieces of pork you can make **Pecan Pork**; just cook the pork for 4 minutes each batch. This is a nice, quick one-dish meal that pleases.

CHICKEN: Calories—343; Carb—11.8; Fat—16.0; Chol—97.0; Pro—37.9; Fib—1.0

PORK: Calories—422; Carb—11.8; Fat—21.1; Chol—58.7; Pro—25.8; Fib—1.0

CRANBERRY CHICKEN

2 whole (12 oz. each) chicken breasts, skinned and cut in half
3 tbsp. diet margarine
1 clove garlic, minced
1 tsp. shallots, minced
1/2 cup sweet red bell pepper, julienned
1/2 cup sweet yellow bell pepper, julienned
1 tsp. salt
1/2 tsp. black pepper
1/4 tsp. red pepper
1/4 tsp. garlic powder
1/2 cup dry vermouth
1/4 cup cranberry sauce, whole berries
1/2 cup plain yogurt, low-fat
1 tbsp. fresh parsley, minced

Take the chicken breasts and check to be sure that there are no tendons or excess fat remaining. Add the margarine to a large, heavy skillet over medium heat and let it melt. When it begins to smoke, add the breasts and cook for 2 minutes on the first side, then turn them over and brown the other side for 3 minutes. When you turn the breasts over, add the garlic and shallots and sauté them with the chicken.

When the breasts are browned, add the red and yellow bell peppers and sauté them for 1 minute. Season with salt, black pepper, red pepper, and garlic powder, then add the wine. Cover and cook for 15 minutes. Add the cranberry sauce, stir into the liquid, baste the chicken, and continue cooking for another 15 minute period.

When the time has passed, remove the chicken to a warm platter and add the yogurt to the skillet. Blend it in well and let it simmer for 2 minutes, but do not boil. Return the chicken to the skillet and add the parsley. Simmer for 1 minute; arrange each breast on four warm serving plates and spoon the sauce over the top, then serve hot. Serves 4.

Lagniappe: This dish can be made completely in advance and refrigerated. It cannot be frozen. When you reheat, do so over a very low fire and just let it simmer, stirring often. Take great care not to boil; it will cause the sauce to curdle and separate. This dish can be served with noodles, potatoes, or rice.

Calories — 418; Carb — 9.4; Fat — 11.2; Chol — 147.3; Pro — 55.4; Fib — 0.6

CHICKEN AND THE SEA

3 whole (12 oz. each)
   chicken breasts,
   skinned and boned
1 cup yogurt, at room
   temperature
1/2 tsp. sweet basil
1/2 tsp. thyme
1/2 tsp. tarragon
1/2 tsp. rosemary
1 tsp. garlic powder
1 tsp. salt
1 tsp. paprika
1 tsp. Dijon mustard

2 cups corn flakes
vegetable oil spray, butter
   flavor
2 tbsp. diet margarine,
   melted
1 cup boiled shrimp,
   peeled and deveined
1/4 cup ripe black olives,
   chopped
1 tbsp. pimento, chopped
1 tbsp. fresh parsley,
   minced

Preheat the oven to 350 degrees. Cut the chicken breasts in half right where the breast bone met the skin. Mix together the yogurt, spices, and Dijon mustard. Dredge each breast half in the seasoned yogurt. Take the corn flakes and crush them well. Roll the dipped chicken in the corn flake crumbs and arrange on a 2-quart casserole that has been sprayed with the vegetable oil spray. Drizzle 1 teaspoon of melted margarine on each piece of chicken and bake at 350 degrees for 45 minutes.

While the chicken is baking, chop the shrimp into large pieces, and mix the shrimp, black olives, pimento, and parsley with the yogurt that remained and blend together well. When the chicken has cooked 45 minutes, turn it over and bake for 15 more minutes at 350 degrees. Spoon the shrimp-yogurt mixture over the chicken and return to the oven to bake for 10 minutes longer. Serve hot. Serves 6.

Lagniappe: You can bake this chicken in advance and refrigerate for later use, but do not freeze. You don't have to worry about the crunch being gone, because it is gone once you add the yogurt-shrimp mixture to the top anyway. It will keep in the refrigerator for 2 days. I like to add the yogurt-shrimp mixture to the top and then refrigerate without the last 10 minute baking. When you are ready to serve, just bake for 12 minutes at 350 degrees or until heated through. This is a real company dish . . . it's almost a shame that it isn't harder to make!

Calories—363; Carb—12.5; Fat—10.6; Chol—172.8; Pro—59.5; Fib—0.3

BAKED CHICKEN ROSE BELLE

1 slice light bread, whole
   wheat (40 calories a
   slice)
1 tsp. salt
1/2 tsp. red pepper
1/4 tsp. black pepper
1/4 tsp. white pepper
1 tsp. paprika
1/2 tsp. garlic powder
1/2 tsp. sweet basil

1/4 tsp. rosemary, crushed
6 tsp. Butter Buds
1 large (3 lb.) fryer, cut
   into serving pieces
1/4 cup dry vermouth
1/4 cup chicken stock or
   chicken broth
2 tbsp. fresh parsley
1/2 tbsp. diet margarine,
   melted

Turn the oven on to 200 degrees. Take the slice of bread, put it in the oven, and just let it dry out. Mix together well the seasonings and the Butter Buds. Use the mixture to season the chicken pieces. Place the pieces skin side up in a large, shallow baking dish, and pour the wine and chicken stock around the sides of the chicken pieces. Bake at 350 degrees for 40 minutes.

Take the bread from the oven and run it through a food processor to make bread crumbs. Toss the bread crumbs with the fresh parsley and the melted margarine and sprinkle it on top of the chicken when it has baked for 40 minutes. Return to the oven and bake for 20 more minutes. Baste the chicken 3 or 4 times with the liquid during the cooking process. Serve hot. Serves 6.

Lagniappe: While this is best eaten just after it is cooked, you can refrigerate and even freeze and serve later. Just thaw in the refrigerator and reheat in the oven at 300 degrees. You can serve the chicken with noodles, if you like, and use the pan drippings as a light sauce.

Calories — 335; Carb — 2.9; Fat — 7.7; Chol — 130.0; Pro — 48.1; Fib — 0.2

Vegetables

This is the section where the recipes allow you to really eat your fill. Vegetables do so much for flavor, color, and texture. By their very nature, they are low in calories. This enables you to serve large portions and still keep the calorie count low. Vegetables add so much variety in taste. I have stressed throughout this book that variety in cooking and eating will go a long way toward keeping you on track. If you eat plenty of vegetables, you will get your fill quickly and remain so longer. You will also get a great deal of the vitamins and minerals your body needs from vegetables; getting these from natural sources insures a better result than taking supplements.

Don't just use vegetables as a complement to meat dishes. The research strongly suggests you have a number of meatless meals during the week. Vegetables are the best way to get food value without serving meat. Plan a few meatless meals during the week. Fix a three or five vegetable plate for dinner, and you'll find that the tastes and colors will blend to create a fine dining experience.

Whenever possible, select fresh vegetables. You get more for your money in food value and in taste. Stay with vegetables that are in season, because chances are they are fresher. Find out from your market what day it receives fresh produce. Then plan to shop on that day, since you can better protect the quality of the vegetable in your own refrigerator, away from "picking" hands. Plan your menus for the week or at least for several days. It will help prevent trips to the store and also allow you to get fresh vegetables for the week each time you shop.

There is a great variety of produce available to us today. Almost every trip to the supermarket will yield surprises. Produce that once was impossible to find is now available almost every day and at competitive prices. Take advantage of this variety. It helps to be able to offer new and exciting vegetables with your meals. Be creative! Experiment with new things. You may just make your new favorite dish. When you become a creative vegetable cook, you will be a chef.

Vegetables scare people, but nothing could be easier to prepare. Our number one mistake is overcooking. Follow the recipes carefully and you will succeed. Once you are successful, then you can branch out and create dishes of your own. Get excited about working with vegetables and you will excite all who dine with you.

LEMON ASPARAGUS

1 1/2 lb. fresh asparagus, tender	2 tbsp. luke warm water
water for steaming	1 tsp. lemon rind, yellow only
1/2 cup light mayonnaise	1/2 tbsp. dry vermouth
1 1/2 tbsp. fresh lemon juice	1/4 tsp. sweet basil
	1/8 tsp. Tabasco sauce

Cut off the tough ends of the asparagus, just where a sharp knife begins to meet some resistance. Using a vegetable peeler, peel the outer scales. Hold the spear end nearest you and work with the peeler away from you. This will assist in making the asparagus very tender.

Put the asparagus, spears up, in a steamer that has a small amount of water on the bottom (about 1/2 inch). Bring the water to a boil in the steamer over high heat and let it boil for exactly 1 minute. Then turn the heat off, letting the steamer remain on the burner.

While the asparagus is steaming, you can make the lemon sauce. In a small saucepan over low heat, add the remaining ingredients. Using a wire whisk, blend together well and cook for 2 or 4 minutes or until completely heated through. Be sure to stir constantly with the whisk to prevent sticking. When ready, remove the asparagus from the steamer; arrange on your serving plate and spoon the sauce over the asparagus. Serve at once. Serves 6 to 8.

Lagniappe: This is an easy and delicious vegetable. It always looks nice on any plate, adding color to meats. About the only thing you can do in advance is trim and wash the asparagus.

You can substitute 1 1/2 pounds of Brussels sprouts for the asparagus and make **Lemon Brussels Sprouts** or you can substitute 2 medium bunches of broccoli to make **Lemon Broccoli.** For both dishes, the sauce remains the same and should be more than enough to cover.

FOR SIX SERVINGS: Calories—80; Carb—6.0; Fat—5.6; Chol—7.0; Pro—3.7; Fib—1.0

FOR EIGHT SERVINGS: Calories-60; Carb-4.5; Fat-4.2; Chol-5.3; Pro-2.8; Fib-0.8

ARTICHOKE ASPIC

2 cups Tabasco Bloody
   Mary Mix
1 can (8 1/2 oz.) artichoke
   hearts, drained and
   coarsely chopped
1/4 cup lemon juice
1/2 tsp. garlic powder
1/2 tsp. onion powder
1 tsp. Worcestershire
   sauce

1 tsp. vinegar
1 tbsp. unflavored gelatin
1/2 tsp. salt
1/2 tsp. sweet basil
1 tbsp. fresh parsley,
   minced
2 packages (.3 oz.) lemon
   Sugar Free Jell-O
1/3 cup boiling water
2 cubes ice

Heat together all the ingredients, except the last three, in a medium saucepan over medium heat until the gelatin is dissolved and the mixture comes to a low boil. Simmer together for 3 minutes. Remove from the heat and set aside.

Mix the lemon Sugar Free Jell-O with the boiling water until it dissolves, then add the ice and stir until it is melted. Add to the tomato mixture that has cooled somewhat. Mix together well. Pour into eight lightly greased individual gelatin molds. Let chill until firmly set. Serve chilled. Serves 8.

Lagniappe: This recipe keeps well refrigerated for about 3 days. This gives you plenty of latitude in preparation. It makes a nice salad, especially when you need something light but interesting. Serve it on lettuce leaves, garnished with lemon wedges, or on a bed of mixed greens.

Calories — 30; Carb — 5.2; Fat — 0.2; Chol — Trace; Pro — 6.0; Fib — 0.4

QUICK ASPARAGUS CASSEROLE

1 lb. fresh asparagus,
   trimmed and washed
cold water to cover
1 tsp. salt
1/4 tsp. black pepper
1/4 tsp. white pepper
1/2 tsp. Tabasco sauce
2 medium green onions,
   chopped
1 cup Ritz cracker crumbs
2 large eggs, lightly beaten
1/4 cup bell peppers, diced
1/4 cup diced pimento

1/4 cup parsley, minced
1 tbsp. celery, minced
1 clove garlic, minced
1 cup milk
1/4 cup butter, unsalted
1/2 cup American cheese,
   grated
1/2 cup Swiss cheese,
   grated
1/8 cup dry white wine
4 very thin slices lemon for
   garnish

Preheat the oven to 400 degrees. Place the asparagus in a large saucepot and cover with cold water. Place on high heat and bring to a boil; reduce the heat to a simmer. Cook for 4 minutes; remove from the heat and drain. Reserve three nice stems for use as a garnish.

In a large mixing bowl, combine the asparagus and all the remaining ingredients and mix together well. Pour into a buttered 9-inch baking dish and bake at 400 degrees for 30 minutes. Garnish with the three stems (that were reserved) and lemon circles. Serve hot. Serves 6 to 8.

Lagniappe: This dish may be made in advance and refrigerated or frozen for later use. For an even easier method of making this dish, you may use a large can (15 or 16 ounces) of asparagus. Just proceed from the mixing of the ingredients.

Calories — 270; Carb — 12.2; Fat — 19.8; Chol — 99.4; Pro — 11.4; Fib — 0.9

EASY VEGETABLE CASSEROLE

1 head broccoli, washed, trimmed and cut into short spears
1 head cauliflower, washed, trimmed and cut into florets
3/4 lb. Brussels sprouts, washed and trimmed
1/2 lb. carrots, washed and cut into 1-inch pieces
1/2 lb. boiling onions, skin removed
2 stalks celery, washed and cut into 1-inch pieces
cold water to cover
1 cup dry vermouth
1 bay leaf
1 1/2 tsp. salt

1/2 lb. mushrooms, washed and cut into halves
2 cans (10 3/4 oz.) cream of mushroom soup
1 tsp. Tabasco sauce
1 tbsp. Worcestershire sauce
1/4 tsp. sweet basil
1/4 cup fresh parsley, minced
1/4 tsp. dry hot mustard
1/8 tsp. ginger
1/4 cup Cheddar cheese, grated
1/4 cup Swiss cheese, grated
1/8 cup bread crumbs
1 tsp. paprika

In a large stockpot, add the broccoli, cauliflower, Brussels sprouts, carrots, onions, and celery. Cover with cold water; add the vermouth, bay leaf, and salt and place over high heat until the liquid comes to a hard boil. Boil for 1 minute, turn off heat, cover, and let stand in the hot water for 10 minutes. Remove the vegetables and let them drain.

In a large mixing bowl, add the remaining ingredients up to but not including the cheese. Mix well with the vegetables and pour into a large 4-quart buttered casserole. Sprinkle evenly with the two cheeses, then lightly coat with bread crumbs. Garnish with the paprika and bake at 350 degrees for 15 to 20 minutes, or until the cheese is melted and the sauce begins to bubble. Serve hot. Serves 8.

Lagniappe: This dish may be made in advance and refrigerated for up to 2 days before use. Do not freeze. If you want, you can use all frozen vegetables to make this dish. You will lose a lot in quality and freshness, but you will save time. Just prepare the vegetables according to package directions, but be sure to add the vermouth and bay leaf while cooking.

Calories — 176; Carb — 22.2; Fat — 9.5; Chol — 33.2; Pro — 9.5; Fib — 2.7

GLAZED GINGER BEETS

3 tbsp. diet margarine
3 tbsp. brown sugar, dark and firmly packed
3 cups beets, peeled, sliced and cooked
3 tbsp. fresh lemon juice
3 tbsp. red wine vinegar

1/4 tsp. Tabasco sauce
1 tbsp. cornstarch
1/2 tsp. fresh grated lemon peel
1 tsp. fresh grated ginger
1/4 tsp. salt
1/2 tsp. dry hot mustard

In a large saucepan over medium heat, melt the margarine. When melted, add the brown sugar and cook for 2 minutes, constantly stirring. Add the beets, turn the heat to low, and continue to cook for 3 more minutes, stirring constantly. In a small bowl, combine the lemon juice, red wine vinegar, Tabasco sauce, and cornstarch. Mix until the cornstarch is dissolved. Pour over the beets and heat until it boils. Continue to cook and stir constantly until the mixture thickens. Add the lemon peel, ginger, salt, and dry hot mustard; blend in well. Remove from the heat and let stand for 3 to 5 minutes, then serve. You can also refrigerate and serve chilled. Serves 8.

Lagniappe: This is a good make-ahead dish. In fact, refrigerating lets the flavors blend better. You can keep this dish for up to 3 days in the refrigerator, but watch out for snitchers! Do not freeze.

Calories — 105; Carb — 20.6; Fat — 2.6; Chol — Trace; Pro — 0.9; Fib — 0.5

FRESH GREEN BEANS ROMERO

1 1/2 lb. fresh green beans
1 cup white onions,
    coarsely chopped
2 cups water
1/2 tsp. salt
1/2 strip thinly sliced
    bacon
4 tsp. Butter Buds

2 tbsp. fresh parsley,
    minced
1/8 tsp. Tabasco sauce
1/4 tsp. white pepper
3 tbsp. plain yogurt,
    low-fat
1 tsp. fresh lemon juice

Clean the beans well with cold water and snap them in half. Pull off any strings that they may have. Put the beans and the onions into a large saucepan that has a cover, then add the water, salt, and bacon. Bring to a hard boil, then reduce to a simmer. Cook for 6 minutes, covered. Remove from the heat and drain the beans of their liquid, but reserve the liquid. Take 4 tablespoons of the liquid and bring it to a boil. Remove from the heat and add the Butter Buds, parsley, Tabasco, and white pepper. Stir until the Butter Buds are dissolved.

In the large saucepan that you cooked the beans in, mix the seasoned liquid back with the beans and place over low heat. Simmer very low, stirring often, for 1 minute. Remove from the heat and add the yogurt and lemon juice. Serve at once. Serves 6.

Lagniappe: This is a quick fresh green bean recipe. You can completely cook up to the adding of the seasonings to the liquid, and refrigerate until you are ready to serve. To continue, just follow from that point in the recipe. You can also freeze the beans after they have simmered for the 6 minutes with the onions. Remember to freeze them with their cooking liquids, so you will be able to continue the recipe as above. But anytime you use fresh vegetables, you get the most out of them right after cooking.

Calories — 69; Carb — 10.7; Fat — 1.7; Chol — 2.3; Pro — 5.8; Fib — 3.5

GREEN BEANS ROSEMARY

1 lb. fresh green beans
1 1/4 cup water
1/2 strip raw bacon,
  chopped
1/4 tsp. Tabasco sauce
2 tsp. fresh rosemary (or 1
  tsp. dry)
1 medium yellow onion,
  coarsely chopped

1 medium fresh tomato,
  skinned and coarsely
  chopped
1 tbsp. fresh lemon juice
1/4 tsp. fresh ground black
  pepper
1/2 tsp. salt

Wash the green beans well with cold water. Remove the strings and snap the beans in half. Put the beans, water, bacon, Tabasco sauce, fresh rosemary, and onion into a medium saucepan over high heat. Bring to a boil, then reduce the heat to a simmer and simmer 15 minutes, covered. Add the tomato, lemon juice, black pepper, and salt; mix together well and cook for 3 minutes with the cover on. Remove from the heat, stir, let the beans sit for 2 minutes to allow all the flavors to blend, and serve. Serves 6.

Lagniappe: This is another quick vegetable. You can clean the beans ahead of time and set them in the refrigerator until you are ready to serve. It is possible to completely cook this dish and refrigerate or freeze. You will lose some texture, vitamins, and flavor, but not enough to worry about. As with any fresh vegetable, it is always better when eaten right after cooking, but with today's lifestyle this is not always possible. Just thaw it in the refrigerator and either heat in a pan on the stovetop until heated through or, even better, heat it in the microwave (that's about all I like the microwave for— reheating).

If you are watching cholesterol closely, you can leave out the bacon strip and add 1 tablespoon of diet margarine; the calorie count will also be a little less. If you want the bacon taste without the cholesterol, just use the artificial bacon bits for flavoring.

Calories—43; Carb—7.3; Fat—1.3; Chol—10.0; Pro—2.0; Fib—1.7

LIMA BEANS
IN CREAM SAUCE

1 can (17 oz.) baby lima
  beans
1 tbsp. diet margarine
1/2 cup white onions,
  chopped
1 tbsp. celery, minced
1 clove garlic, minced
1/2 tsp. flour

3 tsp. Butter Buds
1/4 tsp. Tabasco sauce
1 tsp. white
  Worcestershire sauce
2 tbsp. sour cream
2 tbsp. fresh parsley,
  minced

Drain the beans of their liquid, but reserve 4 tablespoons of the liquid for later use. In a saucepan over medium heat, melt the margarine. When the margarine begins to smoke, add the onions, celery, and garlic and sauté for 2 minutes. Add the flour and cook for 2 more minutes. Add the 4 tablespoons of liquid from the beans and blend in. Add the Butter Buds, Tabasco sauce, and Worcestershire sauce and mix together well. Add the drained beans, reduce the heat to low, and cook the beans for 2 minutes, stirring often. Add the sour cream and parsley and blend in. Let the sauce come to a low boil, stir, and serve at once. Serves 4.

Lagniappe: Don't do this in advance! It is easy to make and so much better if eaten right after it is cooked. You can use this recipe and substitute speckled butter beans for the limas and make **Speckled Butter Beans in Cream Sauce.** You can use imitation sour cream in this recipe or even low-fat plain yogurt.

Calories — 109; Carb — 12.6; Fat — 2.9; Chol — 2.7; Pro — 4.5; Fib — 1.5

SNOW PEAS WITH
WATER CHESTNUTS

1 tbsp. peanut oil
1 1/4 lb. fresh snow pea
   pods, with ends snapped
   off
1 tbsp. green onions,
   chopped
1 tbsp. bell pepper,
   chopped
1 can (6 oz.) water
   chestnuts, sliced and
   drained

1/4 cup chicken stock or
   chicken broth
2 tsp. soy sauce
1 tsp. salt
1/8 tsp. Tabasco sauce
1 tbsp. toasted sesame
   seeds

Heat a medium skillet over medium-high heat until hot, then add the peanut oil. When the oil starts to smoke, add the fresh snow peas, green onions, and bell pepper and sauté for 3 minutes, stirring constantly. Add the water chestnuts, chicken stock, soy sauce, salt, and Tabasco. Bring the liquid to a boil, then reduce to a simmer and cover. Simmer for 2 1/2 to 3 minutes. Sprinkle with the toasted sesame seeds and serve at once. Serves 6.

Lagniappe: This is such a quick recipe, you would not want to make it in advance. And if you did, you would destroy the freshness and crispness of the pods. This colorful dish will boost the appearance of your entree. It is so easy, you will wonder how it can taste so good!

Calories — 95; Carb — 15.4; Fat — 3.4; Chol — 0.2; Pro — 4.7; Fib — 1.2

BEETS MY WAY

2 cups beets, sliced
1/4 cup white vinegar
1/4 tsp. Tabasco sauce

1/2 tsp. salt
1 tsp. black pepper
1/2 tsp. sweet basil

Mix all ingredients together well and refrigerate the beets, covered, for at least 3 hours. Serve chilled. Serves 4.

Lagniappe: You can make this dish up to 3 days in advance, and keep stored in the refrigerator. I like to keep some ready for snacks. One or two slices really can help kill an appetite. They can be eaten like a pickle chip.

Calories — 83; Carb — 19.3; Fat — 0.5; Chol — Trace; Pro — 1.1; Fib — 0.7

STUFFED TOMATOES

3 medium tomatoes, red and firm
2 tbsp. diet margarine
1/2 cup white onions, chopped
1/4 cup green pepper, chopped
1/4 cup celery, minced
2 cloves garlic, minced
4 large mushrooms, minced
1/4 tsp. Tabasco sauce

6 large ripe black olives, chopped
6 large stuffed green olives, chopped
2 tbsp. Romano cheese, grated
2 tbsp. Parmesan cheese, grated
1/4 cup Italian seasoned bread crumbs
1/2 tsp. sweet basil
vegetable oil spray

Preheat the oven to 400 degrees. Wash the tomatoes well and trim off each end to make a flat bottom. Cut the tomatoes in half and scoop out about 3/8-inch of pulp from each half. Set the pulp aside for later use. Dry the inside of the halves with paper towels and set them aside.

In a large, heavy skillet over medium heat, melt the margarine. When melted, sauté the onions, green pepper, celery, and garlic for 5 minutes. While the sautéing is in progress, in a small saucepan over medium heat, add the reserved tomato pulp and reduce the pulp to half the volume, then set aside for later use.

When the onions are done, add the mushrooms and Tabasco sauce and sauté for 2 more minutes. Add the reduced tomato pulp and the remaining ingredients, except for the vegetable oil spray; blend together well. It should make a paste. Spread the paste evenly in the tomato halves, place the tomatoes in a shallow casserole that has been sprayed with the vegetable oil spray, and bake at 400 degrees for 20 to 25 minutes. The top should be brown and the sides soft, yet firm enough to hold their shape. Serve hot. Serves 6.

Lagniappe: This recipe can be made completely up to the baking point and the stuffed unbaked tomatoes can be refrigerated for up to 3 days. Simply place on the baking casserole and bake according to directions. This is an easy dish that will brighten up almost any entree. It complements nicely a green vegetable.

If you would like to use this as an entree, there are a couple of changes that can be made. To make **Shrimp Stuffed Tomatoes,** simply add 1 1/2 cups of boiled shrimp, peeled, deveined and chopped, to the recipe when you add the chopped mushrooms. You would serve a whole tomato per serving so the recipe would serve 3. To make **Chicken Stuffed Tomatoes,** just add 2 cups of baked chicken breast, boned, skinned and chopped coarsely, to the recipe when the mushrooms are added. Serving size would also be a whole tomato per serving so the recipe would serve 3. Let your mind run wild with this recipe and create your own favorite stuffed tomato!

REGULAR STUFFED TOMATO: Calories — 120; Carb — 9.0; Fat — 7.3; Chol — 6.2; Pro — 3.0; Fib — 1.1

SHRIMP STUFFED TOMATOES: Calories — 145; Carb — 9.4; Fat — 7.6; Chol — 43.7; Pro — 7.7; Fib — 1.1

CHICKEN STUFFED TOMATOES: Calories — 168; Carb — 9.0; Fat — 8.3; Chol — 30.5; Pro — 11.9; Fib — 1.1

BROCCOLI VERMOUTH

1 large head fresh broccoli	1/2 tsp. salt
1 tbsp. olive oil	1/8 tsp. Tabasco sauce
1 1/2 tbsp. diet margarine	1/4 tsp. fresh ground black
2 cloves garlic, minced	pepper
1/4 cup onions, chopped	2 tbsp. fresh lemon juice
1 tbsp. celery, chopped	1 tbsp. fresh parsley,
1 cup dry vermouth	minced

Wash and trim the broccoli, then chop it into bite-size pieces. Set aside for later use. In a large saucepan that has a cover, heat the olive oil and margarine over medium heat until it starts to smoke. Add the garlic, onions, and celery and sauté for 2 minutes. Add the broccoli (be careful, it may splatter the oil) and sauté for 2 minutes. Add the vermouth, salt, Tabasco, black pepper, and lemon juice; stir together. Bring to a boil, then reduce to a simmer. Let it simmer for 2 minutes, then cover and simmer for 6 more minutes. Remove from the heat and drain the broccoli, reserving the liquid. Put the broccoli in a serving dish and keep it warm until ready to serve. Return the vermouth liquid to the heat and reduce it by half. Pour the liquid over the broccoli, sprinkle with the fresh parsley, and serve hot. Serves 6.

Lagniappe: This is really different for broccoli. The vermouth adds a whole new depth and almost creates a new vegetable. You have to try this to appreciate it! Sorry, this can't be done in advance, except for chopping the broccoli, but it is easy, anyway. This is a nice green vegetable to add to a plate in need of color.

You can substitute one pound of Brussels sprouts for the broccoli to make **Brussels Sprouts Vermouth.** The only other change you need to make is to simmer the sprouts for 8 minutes instead of the 6 with the broccoli.

BROCCOLI: Calories — 69; Carb — 6.3; Fat — 4.1; Chol — Trace; Pro — 3.2; Fib — 1.3

BRUSSELS SPROUTS: Calories — 78; Carb — 6.6; Fat — 4.2; Chol — Trace; Pro — 3.5; Fib — 1.4

ORANGE CARROTS

3 cups carrots, julienned
water for steamer
3 tbsp. diet margarine
3 tbsp. brown sugar, light
  and firmly packed
1/2 cup orange juice,
  unsweetened

3 tbsp. fresh lemon juice
1 tbsp. cornstarch
1/2 tsp. fresh grated
  orange peel
1/4 tsp. salt
1/4 tsp. dry hot mustard
1 tbsp. orange marmalade

Put the carrots into a steamer, then cover the bottom with 1/2-inch of water and cover. Bring to a boil and when the steam begins to rise strongly, time 1 minute. Remove from the heat and let the carrots stay in the steamer for 5 minutes.

In a large saucepan over medium heat, melt the margarine. When melted, add the brown sugar and cook for 2 minutes, constantly stirring. Add the carrots, turn the heat to low, and continue to cook for 3 more minutes, stirring constantly.

In a small bowl, combine the orange juice, lemon juice, and cornstarch. Mix until the cornstarch is dissolved. Pour over the carrot mixture and heat until it boils. Continue to cook and stir constantly until the mixture thickens. Add the orange peel, salt, dry hot mustard, and marmalade and blend in until the marmalade is dissolved. Remove from the heat and let the mixture cool, then cover and refrigerate for at least 2 hours. Serve cold or reheat and serve hot. Serves 6.

Lagniappe: Here's a vegetable for those who like make-ahead dishes. Not only can you make this ahead of time, but you must; letting it refrigerate blends the flavors together. You can keep this dish for up to 3 days in the refrigerator, that is if no one finds out it's there! Do not freeze this dish. I really can't decide which way I like it best, hot or cold.

Calories — 81; Carb — 15.8; Fat — 3.2; Chol — Trace; Pro — 0.8; Fib — 0.6

BROCCOLI-WALNUT RICE

1 tbsp. peanut oil
1/2 cup walnuts, coarsely
  chopped
1 head broccoli, chopped
1/2 cup green onions,
  chopped
1 tbsp. celery, chopped
1 tbsp. bell pepper,
  chopped
1 clove garlic, minced

1/2 cup chicken stock or
  chicken broth
1/8 cup dry sherry
2 tbsp. soy sauce
1/4 tsp. Tabasco sauce
1/2 tsp. salt
1 tbsp. fresh parsley,
  minced
2 1/2 cups cooked white
  rice

Heat a large skillet that has a cover over medium high heat until it is hot; add the peanut oil. When the oil begins to smoke, add the walnuts and sauté until lightly browned, about 3 minutes; stir often. Remove the walnuts from the pan and add the broccoli, green onions, celery, bell pepper, and garlic to the skillet; sauté for 4 minutes. Add the chicken stock, sherry, soy sauce, and Tabasco sauce. Bring to a full boil, then reduce the heat to a simmer and cook for 2 minutes. Add the salt, rice, and fresh parsley and mix in well. Cover and simmer for 2 more minutes. Remove from the heat and let the dish stand for 5 minutes. Toss with a fork to fluff; add the sautéed walnuts, then serve at once. Serves 8.

Lagniappe: This dish can be made in advance of serving. It does not really freeze well, but I have frozen it with fair success. You can keep it in the refrigerator for a few days before serving. It is a little tricky to bring it back to serving temperature unless you use a microwave. Just cover tightly with plastic wrap (don't forget to put a few holes in the middle of the wrap to let steam escape) and put at 80 percent power for 3 minutes. Shake the rice around a bit after 2 minutes, then continue to cook for 1 more minute. If you want to reheat on the stove, just add a little chicken stock or broth to a skillet and add the Broccoli-Walnut Rice to the pan and cover; heat at medium, stirring often, until it is heated through. This makes a very colorful addition to many entrees and the food value and calorie count is good.

Calories — 144; Carb — 20.2; Fat — 6.9; Chol — 0.4; Pro — 5.1; Fib — 1.3

CAULIFLOWER PARMESAN

2 cups water
1 tsp. fresh oregano (or 1/4
  tsp. dried)
3 cloves garlic, chopped
1 head cauliflower
1 tsp. salt
1/4 tsp. Tabasco sauce

1 medium lemon, juice
  only
2 tbsp. Parmesan cheese,
  fresh grated
1 tbsp. fresh parsley,
  minced

In a large saucepot over high heat, add the water, oregano, and garlic. Bring to a full boil, then cover, reduce the heat to a low simmer, and simmer for 10 minutes. While the water is simmering, wash the cauliflower and cut into florets. Add the cauliflower florets, salt, and Tabasco sauce to the simmered garlic water, cover, and simmer for 15 minutes or until tender. Remove from the heat and drain the cauliflower well. Place the cauliflower in a nice serving dish and sprinkle with the fresh lemon juice, Parmesan cheese, and fresh parsley. Serve at once. Serves 6.

Lagniappe: Tasty and easy—that describes this dish. Don't make it in advance and don't freeze. You can trim the cauliflower in advance without any harm to the dish. This great, light vegetable goes with almost any meat. The Parmesan seems to pull out the cauliflower flavor and really complement it.

Calories — 33; Carb — 5.0; Fat — 0.7; Chol — 1.0; Pro — 2.7; Fib — 1.0

EASY FRESH BROCCOLI

2 heads fresh broccoli
1 gal. cold water
2 tsp. corn oil
1 tsp. salt

1/2 medium lemon, cut in
half
3 whole green
peppercorns, crushed

Cut the broccoli into serving-size pieces. You should get enough broccoli to serve 8 people. I like to trim off the bottom hard pieces, then split the large pieces right in half. This will allow the broccoli to lie flat on the plate. Add the remaining ingredients into a large pot and bring to a boil. Start the pot boiling about 30 minutes before you wish to eat. When you are 20 minutes away from eating, drop the broccoli into the boiling water and boil for exactly 1 minute, then remove from the heat and let stand for 19 minutes. When you are ready to serve, remove the stems from the hot water, drain on a paper towel, and serve. Serves 8.

Lagniappe: This is the best way to serve broccoli when you want it to be ready and perfect for your meals. Steaming may taste better, but if everything doesn't go just right, you blow it! Also, the little amount of oil added to the water will keep your broccoli a beautiful dark green. You can sauce the broccoli with the Light Butter Sauce or Hollandaise Light found in this book (see index for recipes). Or you can eat just as they are. They have a fresh flavor that speaks for itself.

Calories — 36; Carb — 4.5; Fat — 1.1; Chol — 0.0; Pro — 3.1; Fib — 1.5

STEWED POTATOES PATRICIA

1 lb. white potatoes
1 gal. water
1/2 tsp. salt
1 tbsp. diet margarine
1 medium white onion,
  chopped
1 clove garlic, minced
1 tbsp. celery, minced
2 tsp. all-purpose flour

1/3 cup chicken stock or
  chicken broth
2 tsp. Butter Buds
1/2 tsp. salt
1/4 tsp. white pepper
1/4 tsp. black pepper
1/8 tsp. Tabasco sauce
1 medium bay leaf

Wash the potatoes. Add the 1/2 teaspoon of salt to the water and bring to a hard boil. Boil the potatoes for 5 minutes, then let them sit in the hot water for 5 more minutes. Cool, then peel and cut into slices about 3/4-inch thick.

In a heavy, large skillet over medium heat, add the margarine. Sauté the onions, garlic, and celery for 3 minutes, stirring constantly. Add the flour and cook, stirring constantly, until it begins to brown. Let it get to a nice light brown. Add the chicken stock, a little at a time, until it is all blended. Add the remaining ingredients and mix together well. Put the sliced potatoes into the sauce, reduce the heat to simmer, and let the potatoes simmer for 5 minutes. Serve hot. Serves 4.

Lagniappe: You can cook the potatoes in advance and refrigerate, but do not peel them until you are ready to continue cooking. This is a simple but tasty way to serve potatoes, and its sauce is light. They will accompany almost any entree that calls for potatoes. Remember, potatoes are a complex carbohydrate and a good source of energy that is not likely to be stored as fat.

Calories — 100; Carb — 23.6; Fat — 1.7; Chol — 0.4; Pro — 3.7; Fib — 0.8

BRUSSELS SPROUTS BASIL

1 1/2 lb. fresh Brussels
 sprouts, trimmed and
 washed
1 tbsp. fresh basil, minced
 (or 1 tsp. dry)
2 cups water
1/2 tsp. salt
1/4 tsp. Tabasco sauce
1/4 cup celery, sliced into
 1/4-inch pieces

1/4 cup carrots, sliced into
 thin circles
1 tsp. lemon rind,
 yellow only
1 tsp. Butter Buds
1/4 tsp. white pepper
2 1/2 tbsp. fresh lemon
 juice
1 tsp. tarragon vinegar

Put the Brussels sprouts, basil, water, salt, and Tabasco sauce into a large saucepan that has a cover and place over high heat. Bring to a boil, then reduce the heat to simmer and cover. Simmer for 10 minutes, shaking the pan a few times while the sprouts are cooking. Add the celery and carrots and cook for 3 more minutes with the cover off, stirring a few times during the cooking process. Remove from the heat and drain. Sprinkle with the lemon rind, Butter Buds, and white pepper, then toss. Toss again with the lemon juice and tarragon vinegar. Serve at once. Serves 6.

Lagniappe: This is so easy, you won't want to do anything in advance except clean the Brussels sprouts. You can make in advance and freeze or refrigerate for later use, but remember you will lose a little texture and taste. To reheat, just thaw in the refrigerator and heat in the microwave or on top of the stove. Just add a small amount of water and heat over medium heat, covered, shaking the pan constantly until heated through.

You can use this same recipe with asparagus to make **Asparagus Basil,** by substituting 1 1/2 pounds of asparagus for the Brussels sprouts. Be sure to trim the asparagus and shave off the hard scales with a vegetable peeler. You will also need to reduce the 10 minute cooking time to 4 minutes, then follow as above.

BRUSSELS SPROUTS: Calories—44; Carb—8.6; Fat—0.2; Chol—0.0; Pro—3.8; Fib—2.6

ASPARAGUS: Calories—30; Carb—5.9; Fat—0.2; Chol—0.0; Pro—2.5; Fib—1.7

MIXED VEGETABLE
QUICK FRY

2 tbsp. peanut oil
1 clove garlic, minced
1 cup carrots, cut in circles
about 1/2-inch thick
1 cup cauliflower florets
1/4 cup celery, cut in slices
about 1/4-inch thick
1 cup broccoli florets
1 cup yellow squash, cut in
circles about 1/4-inch
thick

2 tbsp. green pepper,
chopped
1 1/2 tbsp. soy sauce
1 tbsp. dry sherry
1/4 tsp. Tabasco sauce
1/4 tsp. sweet basil
1/2 tsp. salt
1/4 tsp. fresh ground black
pepper
1 tbsp. lemon juice

Heat the peanut oil in a heavy pot that has a lid and a handle for shaking it. When the oil begins to smoke, add the garlic and carrots. Sauté for 2 minutes, then add the cauliflower. You may have to put the lid on top to prevent splattering of the oil. Cook for 2 minutes, then add the celery, broccoli, yellow squash, and green pepper; stir around so that all vegetables are coated. Cook over medium-high heat for 3 minutes with the lid on, shaking the pan often to prevent sticking. Stir well, then add the soy sauce, sherry, Tabasco, sweet basil, salt, black pepper, and lemon juice. Stir together well, cover, and cook for 1 more minute. Serve hot at once. Serves 4.

Lagniappe: Here's a quick frying method for vegetables that benefit from crispness. All you can do in advance is chop the vegetables. Their color is striking on almost any plate. You can vary the vegetables used depending on what is available fresh.

Calories — 103; Carb — 7.9; Fat — 3.7; Chol — 1.0; Pro — 3.2; Fib — 1.0

SWEET PEAS SEGURA

1 can (17 oz.) LeSueur sweet peas	**2 tbsp. green onions, minced**
3 tsp. Butter Buds	**1/8 tsp. Tabasco sauce**
1/4 tsp. garlic powder	**1 packet Equal sweetener**

Drain the peas from their liquid, but reserve the juice. Add the peas to a saucepan over medium heat and add 3 tablespoons of the sweet pea liquid. Add all the remaining ingredients except for the Equal sweetener. Bring to a boil, then reduce to simmer and cook for 5 minutes. Remove from the heat, stir a few times, then add the Equal and let it dissolve. Serve at once. Serves 4.

Lagniappe: When it comes to peas, this may be my favorite. Don't let the fact that it comes from a can keep you from trying this dish. No need to make or cook in advance, because there is no work or time involved. You can make in advance and refrigerate, just don't add the Equal until you have reheated over low. Add the Equal just before serving. Green peas add a nice color to most potatoes or noodles.

Calories — 70; Carb — 13.0; Fat — Trace; Chol — 0.0; Pro — 4.1; Fib — 1.5

BOILED POTATOES
SAUCE BOULIGNY

1 lb. new potatoes, small
  red
1 gal. water
1 tsp. salt
4 whole black pepper-
  corns, crushed
3 tsp. Butter Buds

2 whole fresh basil leaves
  (or 1/4 tsp. dried)
3 tbsp. very hot water
1/8 tsp. Tabasco sauce
1 tbsp. fresh parsley,
  minced
1/2 tsp. garlic, minced

Wash the potatoes, but leave the skin on. Put the salt, peppercorns, and basil leaves into the gallon of water. Bring that gallon of water to a hard boil, then drop the potatoes into the pot. Let them boil for 5 minutes. While the potatoes are boiling, mix the remaining ingredients together and blend well until the Butter Buds dissolve. Remove the potatoes from the water with a slotted spoon and let them drain. Put them in a large serving bowl and toss with the sauce. Serve hot. Serves 4.

Lagniappe: This is one of my favorite ways to eat potatoes. You don't add that much to them, but just enough to make them zesty. You can boil them in advance and refrigerate, but they are really better just after they are cooked. Do not freeze. Should you decide to make in advance, store in the refrigerator in the sauce until you are ready to serve. Then just add to a pot and heat over low heat. You can also heat in the microwave at 80 percent power for about 1 1/2 minutes, but you will need to stir them around about halfway through the cooking process. This is a nice low-calorie potato to have with any meat.

Calories — 98; Carb — 20.6; Fat — Trace; Chol — Trace; Pro — 2.6; Fib — 0.8

QUICK SWEET
PUMPKIN LEMOINE

3 cups fresh pumpkin, cut
   into 1/2-inch cubes
vegetable oil spray, butter
   flavor
1 tbsp. diet margarine
1/4 tsp. salt

1/2 tsp. nutmeg
1/2 tsp. ginger
1/4 tsp. cinnamon
1/2 tsp. vanilla extract
2 tsp. Butter Buds
3 packets Equal sweetener

Soak the pumpkin in cold water for 5 minutes. Check to be sure that none of the cubes have pumpkin skin, which will make the dish bitter. Heat a skillet over medium heat until it is hot; remove from the heat and spray with the vegetable oil spray. Return to the heat and add the margarine.

When the margarine melts and begins to smoke, add the pumpkin and sauté over medium heat for 2 minutes, stirring constantly. Add the salt, nutmeg, ginger, and cinnamon and sauté for 2 minutes more. Add the vanilla and Butter Buds and blend in well, stirring over the heat. Remove from the heat and add the Equal. Serve at once. Serves 6.

Lagniappe: Pumpkin is a "good buy" fresh vegetable. You get a lot for your money, especially if you buy it for a flat price and not a per-pound price. You can make this recipe in advance up to the adding of the vanilla, Butter Buds, and Equal. Once the pumpkin is sautéed, it can be refrigerated or frozen for later use. To serve, just thaw in the refrigerator and continue the recipe as above. If you have any leftovers, you cannot reheat them, but the dish is good cold.

Calories — 48; Carb — 4.9; Fat — 1.3; Chol — Trace; Pro — 0.5; Fib — 0.8

SKILLET POTATOES

2 lb. red potatoes, medium
cold water to cover
1 1/2 tsp. salt
1/2 tsp. fresh ground black
pepper

2 tbsp. butter, unsalted
1/2 tsp. Tabasco sauce
1/4 cup fresh parsley,
minced

Wash the potatoes well. Put them in a large pot and cover them with water. Add the salt and fresh ground black pepper and bring the water to a boil. Let it boil for 7 minutes or until the potatoes are tender but not overcooked. Drain the potatoes on paper towels and let them dry. When they are cool, you can easily remove the red skin without taking any of the potato with the skin. Slice them into circles about 1/4-inch thick.

Add the butter to a large skillet and heat over medium heat until the butter melts, then raise the temperature to high and wait for the butter to smoke. Just as the butter starts smoking, add the potatoes. If your skillet is large enough they should all be able to lie flat. Brown well on each side, shaking the pan often as they cook. Add the Tabasco sauce and mix in well. Just about 1 minute before the potatoes are ready to serve, add the fresh minced parsley. Serve hot at once. Serves 6.

Lagniappe: This is an easy, excellent alternative to traditional hash browns for breakfast or an exciting new way to serve potatoes for dinner. Do not freeze. You can boil the potatoes up to 24 hours in advance and proceed with the recipe at a later time. To vary the dish a little, you can add additional flavor (and calories) by adding 1/4 cup of crumbled cooked bacon or diced ham.

Calories—160; Carb—26.7; Fat—4.1; Chol—Trace; Pro—3.5; Fib— 0.9

FRESH SPINACH POUJOUX

1 lb. fresh spinach
1/2 cup white onion,
  chopped
2 tbsp. celery, chopped
1/2 tsp. salt
1 cup cold water
1/4 tsp. Tabasco sauce

1/2 strip thinly sliced
  smoked bacon,
  uncooked
1/2 tsp. chicken bouillon
  granules
2 tsp. Butter Buds

Wash the spinach well under cold water. Place in a medium saucepan over medium heat and add all of the remaining ingredients, except for the Butter Buds. Bring to a hard boil, reduce the heat to simmer, and cover. Cook for 7 minutes or until the spinach is tender. Add the Butter Buds and stir until they are dissolved. Serve at once. Serves 4.

Lagniappe: You can make this dish in advance and either refrigerate or freeze. Do not add the Butter Buds until you are ready to serve. To serve, just thaw in the refrigerator, heat until hot, add the Butter Buds, and serve. You can also put it right from the freezer into the microwave and heat at 30 percent power for 1 minute, then 80 percent power for 1 more minute. This delicious dish is surprisingly easy to prepare.

Calories — 66; Carb — 5.5; Fat — 4.6; Chol — 0.3; Pro — 4.5; Fib — 0.9

MASHED POTATOES

3 medium white baking
  potatoes
water to cover
1 tsp. salt
3 whole black peppercorns
1 packet (4 oz.) Butter
  Buds
1/2 cup hot tap water

1/2 cup milk, whole 3.5%
  fat
1 tbsp. fresh chives,
  snipped
1/2 tsp. salt
1/4 tsp. fresh ground black
  pepper

Wash the potatoes to remove any dirt; cut off any bad spots. Over high heat, in a large pot, add the potatoes and cover them with cold water. Add the teaspoon of salt and the black peppercorns. Bring to a hard boil, then reduce to a low rolling boil. Cook until the potatoes can be pierced through easily with a fork, about 20 minutes. Remove from the heat, drain, and let cool for a few minutes.

Empty the packet of Butter Buds into a large mixing bowl and add the hot tap water. Use a wire whisk and blend the water with the Butter Buds; it will make a nice yellow sauce that looks like melted butter.

Stick one potato with a fork so you can hold it, and use a knife to remove the layer of thin skin; it will come off very easily. Repeat until you have finished all three potatoes. Add the milk, fresh chives, salt, and fresh ground black pepper and mix together well, but do not whip; leave the potatoes lumpy. Serve hot. Serves 6.

Lagniappe: People always make the mistake of thinking that potatoes are high in calories. They are not! In addition, they have complex carbohydrates which are not only good for you, but necessary to anyone who is seriously interested in losing weight. You can make this dish in advance and refrigerate for later use, but I usually only like to do this with its leftovers. A nice way to reheat them is in the microwave; just cover them with plastic wrap, punch a few holes in the center of the plastic to allow steam to escape, and set the microwave on 80 percent power for 2 minutes. You can also reheat in a saucepan, over medium heat, but you will have to stir the potatoes around often to keep them from sticking.

Calories — 111; Carb — 16.6; Fat — 0.7; Chol — 2.8; Pro — 1.8; Fib — 0.3

Desserts

This is my favorite section! No low-calorie cookbook should be without a dessert section. Having a little something sweet just seems to complete a meal and makes you feel as though you have eaten well. One problem with "dieting" is the negative "give-up" syndrome. You are warned over and over about all the things you can't have. Desserts are usually high on the list of "no-no's." My own personal taste lies in the other direction. I like having a sweet after my dinner or at least sometime during the day. It doesn't have to be something fancy, just sweet, tasty, and creative.

The desserts in this section are easy, quick, and eye-catching. The way a dish looks goes a long way toward making that dish special. Take the time necessary to add ambiance to your dishes. Looks are no substitute for taste and never will be, but they can be an enhancement.

Don't limit yourself to the recipes in this book for dessert. Often I will choose something that is already made or packaged, such as cookies. You can look on the package for an exact calorie count. Often one or two cookies will give you all the sweet taste you need for just about 100 calories. Steer clear of a bakery or cookie shop for your sweets. You will not be able to get an accurate calorie count from them and you can really "do yourself in" by frequenting such a place. When it comes to desserts, fix it yourself to be sure of the calorie count or buy only sweets that come with a calorie count and other dietary information. Read the labels to be sure that you are getting exactly what you think you are getting.

To succeed at weight loss, you don't have to do without. You just have to (I know you are tired of hearing it, but I can't say it too many times) COUNT you caloric intake. If you stay within your set limits, there is nothing you can't eat. Keep the sweet side of your weight loss in mind. Have and enjoy your dessert. Plan for it, count it, then ENJOY.

ROYAL PINEAPPLE CREPE

3/4 cup ricotta cheese,
  part-skim
3/4 cup fresh pineapple,
  diced and drained
3 packets Equal sweetener
1/2 tsp. fresh lemon rind
1 tbsp. orange-flavored
  liqueur

1/2 tsp. vanilla extract
4 whole crêpes (see index
  for recipe)
4 tbsp. Cool Whip
  non-dairy topping
4 chunks fresh pineapple,
  about 1-inch square

Mix well all but the last three ingredients. Refrigerate for 2 hours. Spoon one-fourth of the mixture into the center of each crêpe, roll the crêpe up, and place seam-down in the center of a dessert plate. Garnish with the Cool Whip and chunk of fresh pineapple. Serve cold. Serves 4.

Lagniappe: You can make the crêpe filling up to 24 hours in advance and refrigerate. Of course, you can make the crêpes in advance and even freeze them. It won't take you longer than a minute to assemble the dish once the filling and crêpe are prepared. I suggest not rolling the crêpe until right before you are ready to serve, since it looks better.

Calories — 165; Carb — 17.3; Fat — 7.0; Chol — 87.8; Pro — 9.7; Fib — 0.2

LOLLY'S FROZEN
LIME SOUFFLE

3/4 cup water
2 tbsp. fresh lime rind,
    green only
1/4 cup fresh lime juice
1 tbsp. sugar
2 packages (.3 oz. each)
    lime Sugar Free Jell-O

3 large ice cubes
5 large eggs, whites only
1/4 tsp. cream of tartar
2 tbsp. powdered sugar
2 cups Cool Whip
    non-dairy topping

Pour the water, lime rind, lime juice, and sugar into a saucepan and place over medium heat. Bring to a boil, reduce to simmer, and simmer for 5 minutes. Raise the heat once again and bring to a hard boil; remove from the heat and stir in the lime Sugar Free Jell-O. As soon as it is dissolved, add the 3 ice cubes and stir until they melt. Refrigerate until the Jell-O is slightly thick.

Beat the egg whites until they begin to stiffen; add the cream of tartar and powdered sugar a little at a time. Continue to beat the egg whites until they are very stiff. Fold the Cool Whip and egg white together until well blended. Fold this egg white-Cool Whip mixture with the chilled Jell-O until smooth. It will have a nice, light green color. Spoon into eight individual molds, dessert glasses, or wine glasses. Return to the refrigerator and let set until firm. Serve chilled. Serves 8.

Lagniappe: This may be made up to 2 days in advance. After that time it can begin to break apart. Do not freeze. This is a quick and light dessert that is nice after almost any dinner. You don't have to be counting calories to like this!

Calories—87; Carb—9.5; Fat—4.0; Chol—0.0; Pro—2.6; Fib—Trace

BLUEBERRY MOUSSE

1 tbsp. unflavored gelatin
1 cup cold water
1 lb. fresh blueberries
1/2 cup crushed pineap-
  ple, unsweetened
1 package (.3 oz.) rasp-
  berry or black raspberry
  Sugar Free Jell-O

1/2 cup plain yogurt,
  low-fat
1/4 cup powdered sugar
2 cups Cool Whip
  non-dairy topping
vegetable oil spray

Dissolve the unflavored gelatin in the cold water, pour it into a sauce-pan, and heat over medium heat until it comes to a boil. Add the blueberries and crushed pineapple. Leave on the heat for 2 minutes, stirring constantly. Remove from the heat and add the raspberry Sugar Free Jell-O. Mix together until the Jell-O is dissolved. Add the yogurt and powdered sugar and stir in well until the yogurt is blended in. Refrigerate until it begins to set. Fold in the Cool Whip. Spray eight individual molds lightly, with the vegetable oil spray, and chill until set. Unmold and serve chilled. Serves 8.

Lagniappe: This mousse can be made 2 or 3 days ahead of use and kept refrigerated. Remember to cover the bottoms of the molds with plastic wrap to prevent food flavors from being absorbed by the mousse. The way I really like to serve this dish is in little souffle dishes. Take wax paper and make a cuff about 1 1/2-inches high around each souffle and tape it together. Fill each souffle dish about 1 1/4 inches above the top of the souffle. When the mousse is set, carefully cut the wax paper away. This makes an exceptional presentation. The white dish is graced with a crown of blueberries. A really showy yet light dessert.

Calories — 132; Carb — 21.0; Fat — 4.6; Chol — 1.8; Pro — 6.4; Fib — 1.9

BREAD PUDDING

4 slices light bread (40
   calories per slice)
1 1/2 cups skim milk
1/2 cup light packed
   peaches, chopped
1/4 cup raisins

2 large eggs, beaten
3 tbsp. sugar
1 tbsp. honey
1/2 tsp. ground nutmeg
1/2 tsp. cinnamon
1 tsp. vanilla extract

Tear the bread apart and put it into a large mixing bowl. Pour the milk on top of the bread and let it soak for a few minutes, then add the peaches and raisins. Stir together well. Mix remaining ingredients well. Pour the egg mixture into the bread mixture and stir well. Pour into a shallow 1 1/2-quart casserole and place that casserole in a larger pan that has 1 inch of water in it. Bake at 350 degrees for 45 minutes or until a clean knife inserted in the center of the pudding comes out clean. Serve warm or cold. Serves 6.

Lagniappe: This pudding can be made earlier and reheated in the oven or in the microwave. In the oven, heat for 2 minutes at 300 degrees. In the microwave, heat at 80 percent power for 45 seconds. Serve at once. You can top with a little Cool Whip or you can make a light lemon or whiskey sauce. Do not freeze.

Calories — 140; Carb — 24.1; Fat — 2.1; Chol — 92.3; Pro — 6.0; Fib — 0.2

CHOCOLATE MOCHA PUDDING

3 cups skim milk, scalded
1 tsp. instant coffee
1 tbsp. honey
2 1/2 tbsp. cocoa,
  unsweetened
4 tbsp. sugar

1/4 cup cornstarch
1 tsp. Butter Buds
1/4 tsp. salt
1 tbsp. vanilla extract
1 tsp. Tia Maria liqueur or
  other coffee liqueur

Use a medium saucepan over low heat to scald the milk. When the milk is scalded and still warm, mix in the instant coffee and honey well.

Mix together the cocoa, sugar, cornstarch, Butter Buds, and salt. When the scalded milk is cool, mix in the cocoa-cornstarch mixture until it is completely dissolved. Return the saucepan to low heat and cook, stirring constantly, until the mixture is thick. Remove from the heat and stir in the vanilla extract and Tia Maria. Let the mixture cool in the pan for 4 minutes, then spoon into six individual serving dishes. Chill in the refrigerator for at least 2 hours. Serve cold. Serves 6.

Lagniappe: This low-calorie chocolate pudding tastes great. It can be made up to 24 hours in advance and refrigerated until you are ready to serve. If you like, you can serve 1 tablespoon of Cool Whip on top for an additional 13 calories.

Calories — 110; Carb — 23.0; Fat — 0.5; Chol — 2.6; Pro — 5.5; Fib — 0.6

CHOCOLATE MOUSSE

5 squares unsweetened
  chocolate
6 large eggs, separated
1/2 tsp. instant coffee
2 tbsp. hot water
1/4 cup sugar

1/2 tsp. pure vanilla
  extract
8 packets Equal sweetener
2 cups whipped
  evaporated skim milk

In a double boiler over medium heat, melt the chocolate. While the chocolate is melting, take only three of the egg yolks and beat for 1 minute. Add the instant coffee to the hot water and dissolve. Add the coffee mixture to the yolks and blend together well.

Add the yolk-coffee mixture and the sugar to the melted chocolate and mix together well. Cook over low steam in the double boiler for 4 minutes, stirring constantly. The mixture should thicken nicely.

Beat the egg whites until they begin to stiffen. Slowly add the vanilla and Equal; continue to beat until stiff peaks form. Let the egg-chocolate mixture cool a little, then carefully fold it into the beaten egg whites. Fold in the whipped evaporated milk and spoon into dessert dishes or wine glasses. Chill for at least 5 hours. Serve chilled. Serves 10.

Lagniappe: This is the classic dessert, lightened for those who just have to have a special dessert but don't want all the calories. You can make this dessert up to 24 hours in advance and keep refrigerated for serving at a later time. This dessert is always a favorite and will certainly satisfy "chocoholics."

Calories — 161; Carb — 16.0; Fat — 10.8; Chol — 165.2; Pro — 6.8; Fib — 0.4

STRAWBERRY PUDDING

2 cups skim milk
2 tbsp. honey
1 1/2 cups fresh
strawberries, sliced
4 tbsp. sugar
2 tsp. Butter Buds
1/4 tsp. salt

2 tbsp. orange-flavored
liqueur
1 tbsp. fresh lemon juice
3 1/2 tbsp. cornstarch
2 drops red food coloring
1 large egg, slightly beaten
2 tsp. vanilla extract

In a medium saucepan over low heat, add the milk, honey, fresh strawberries, sugar, and Butter Buds. Cook over low heat for 10 minutes, stirring constantly. While cooking the strawberries, mix together the salt, orange liqueur, fresh lemon juice, cornstarch, and red food coloring. Stir until the cornstarch is completely dissolved.

Add the cornstarch mixture to the strawberry mixture and cook, constantly stirring, until the mixture begins to thicken. Add the vanilla and 1/2 cup of the hot strawberry mixture to the beaten egg and mix together well. Pour the egg mixture into the remaining strawberry mixture in the saucepan and continue cooking until the pudding has thickened. Let the mixture cool in the pan for 4 minutes, then spoon into six individual serving dishes. Chill in the refrigerator for at least 2 hours. Serve cold. Serves 6.

Lagniappe: This is a delicious low-calorie strawberry pudding. It can be made up to 24 hours in advance and refrigerated until you are ready to serve. If you like, you can serve 1 tablespoon of Cool Whip on top for an additional 13 calories.

Calories — 148; Carb — 26.7; Fat — 1.2; Chol — 47.0; Pro — 4.1; Fib — 0.7

BLUEBERRIES BOULIGNY

2 tbsp. diet margarine
2 tbsp. light brown sugar
2 tbsp. sugar
1/4 tsp. fresh lemon rind
1/4 tsp. fresh minced
   ginger
1/8 cup blackberry liqueur
1 lb. fresh blueberries,
   washed and stems
   removed

1/4 cup Cognac
1/4 cup cold water
1 tbsp. cornstarch
3 tsp. Butter Buds
3 packets Equal sweetener
4 cups vanilla ice milk

In a large skillet or flambé pan over medium heat, melt the margarine. Add the brown sugar, sugar, lemon rind, and ginger. Sauté for 5 minutes, stirring constantly. Add the blackberry liqueur and stir around until you have a thick sauce. Add the fresh blueberries and cook, stirring constantly, for 4 minutes. Carefully pour in the Cognac and let it heat for a few seconds, then put a match near it and ignite. Flambé the blueberries until the fire goes out on its own. Be careful not to splatter the sauce or you could spread the flame. Just gently shake the pan.

When the flames are gone, mix the Butter Buds, cornstarch, and water, then pour into the blueberry mixture. Stir in well and cook until the sauce thickens nicely. Remove from the heat and add the Equal. Spoon generous amounts equally over 1/2-cup servings of vanilla ice milk. Serve at once. Serves 8.

Lagniappe: At last a dessert sauce that saves. You can make this for your guests and serve, then refrigerate the leftovers for a later treat. Refrigerate for up to 1 week. When you want to serve, spoon cold over the ice milk of your choice. Remember, because the sauce has Equal in it, you cannot reheat. If you don't want to flambé in front of your guests, you can make up to the adding of the

Equal and refrigerate. When you are ready to serve, just warm gently over low heat until hot, remove from the heat, stir in the Equal, and serve. A great topping for your favorite ice milk or frozen yogurt.

Calories — 200; Carb — 32.0; Fat — 4.5; Chol — 9.0; Pro — 3.0; Fib — 1.8

PECAN PUFFS

2 large eggs, whites only
1/3 cup sugar
1/2 tsp. fresh orange rind
1 tsp. vanilla extract
1/4 tsp. cream of tartar

1/4 cup lightly toasted pecans
wax paper for lining cookie sheet

Preheat the oven to 300 degrees. In a large mixing bowl, beat the egg whites until peaks begin to form. Slowly beat in the sugar, orange rind, vanilla, and cream of tartar. Continue beating until stiff peaks form. Carefully fold in the pecans. Line a cookie sheet with the wax paper and spoon about 2 tablespoons of batter at a time onto the wax paper. Bake at 300 degrees for 35 to 40 minutes or until the puffs are lightly browned. Remove carefully from the paper and cool on a baking rack. Makes about 20 large cookies.

Lagniappe: Easy to make and light as a feather! Do not stack the cookies on each other the same day they are made. They may stick together. You can change the nuts in this recipe, if you like, to vary the taste.

PER COOKIE: Calories — 21; Carb — 3.6; Fat — 1.1; Chol — 27.4; Pro — 0.7; Fib — Trace

ON BLUEBERRY ISLAND

vegetable oil spray
4 large eggs, whites only
1/4 tsp. salt
1/4 tsp. cream of tartar
1/8 tsp. ground nutmeg
1/4 tsp. fresh lemon rind,
   grated very fine

1/2 tsp. vanilla extract
3 tbsp. sugar, fine
2 cups fresh blueberries,
   washed
3 tbsp. sugar

Preheat the oven to 300 degrees. Spray the bottom of a cookie sheet with the vegetable oil spray and set the sheet aside. In a large mixing bowl, beat the egg whites with the salt, cream of tartar, and ground nutmeg. As the eggs begin to stiffen, slowly add the lemon rind, vanilla extract, and the first 3 tablespoons of sugar. Beat until stiff. Make six nice, fluffy mounds (islands) on the baking sheet and bake for 15 to 18 minutes at 300 or until the islands are lightly browned. Remove and cool on a wire rack.

Put the blueberries into a food processor or blender and purée, slowly adding the sugar remaining. When the sugar has dissolved, pour the blueberry-purée into a shallow decorative dish. Carefully "float" the meringue islands in the blueberry-purée. Chill for at least 2 hours. Serve chilled. Arrange the island on a sea of blueberry sauce. Serves 6.

Lagniappe: While there really isn't a lot of work to this recipe, it is quite presentable. It is a dessert that is light enough for any meal, yet sweet enough to please. I don't like to let this dish refrigerate for too long. Meringue begins to bead and lose its texture after sitting. Try to use it within 4 to 6 hours. Please be sure that the islands are completely cooled before adding them to the sauce. If they are still warm, it will promote the beading of moisture on the surface of the meringue.

You can use this very recipe with 2 cups of fresh raspberries in the place of the blueberries to make **No Man Is a Raspberry Island.** The humor is free!

Calories — 98; Carb — 22.5; Fat — 0.4; Chol — Trace; Pro — 0.4; Fib — 1.5

MELON BALL MELANGE

2 cups honeydew balls, seeded

2 cups watermelon balls, seeded

1 cup cantelope balls, seeded

2 medium kiwifruit, peeled and thinly sliced

1 tsp. fresh mint leaves, crushed

2 tbsp. fresh lime juice

2 tbsp. orange-flavored liqueur

3 packets Equal sweetener

Mix together the melon balls, kiwifruit, and fresh mint. Arrange in six nice dessert dishes and refrigerate. Mix together the remaining ingredients and chill. When ready to serve, drizzle the liquid over the melon mixture. Serve chilled. Serves 6.

Lagniappe: Don't make this too much in advance of serving. The melon balls will get soggy. You can do it up to 5 hours in advance, which should give you plenty of leeway. This is a fresh, colorful, and very light dessert that will complement almost any meal.

Calories — 78; Carb — 16.4; Fat — 0.5; Chol — 0.0; Pro — 1.0; Fib — 1.0

STRAWBERRY SUNDAE

**1 package (10 oz.) frozen
  strawberries,
  unsweetened, with juice
1 tsp. fresh lemon juice**

**1 tbsp. cornstarch
3 cups vanilla ice milk
6 tbsp. Cool Whip
  non-dairy topping**

Let the strawberries defrost in the refrigerator in a glass bowl. When defrosted, drain the strawberries from the liquid. Mix the strawberry juice, lemon juice, and cornstarch and blend until the cornstarch is dissolved. Heat the juice in a saucepan over medium heat until boiling. Reduce to a simmer and cook until the sauce thickens, about 2 to 3 minutes. Remove from the heat and add the drained berries. Cool in the refrigerator. When cool, spoon 3 tablespoons of the sauce over the ice milk. Garnish with 1 tablespoon of Cool Whip. This recipe makes just over 1 cup of sauce. Serves 6.

Lagniappe: You can make this sauce up to 3 days in advance. It will actually keep a little longer, but the strawberries become too soggy. It is nice over cheesecake or just a plain slice of pound cake. The sauce itself is about 10 calories per tablespoon. Enjoy!

Calories — 136; Carb — 19.1; Fat — 3.9; Chol — 9.0; Pro — 2.9; Fib — 0.6

BAKED LOWER ALASKA

4 pieces shortcake
2 cups vanilla ice milk
8 whole fresh straw-
  berries, cut in slices
2 packets Equal sweetener
4 large eggs, whites only

1/8 tsp. cream of tartar
1 tbsp. sugar
1 tsp. vanilla extract
1 drop green food coloring
4 tsp. brandy

Spread the 4 shortcake pieces on a small tray and place 1/2 cup of the vanilla ice milk on each shortcake. Arrange the fresh strawberry slices on top of the ice milk to cover completely. Sprinkle 1/2 pack of Equal on top of the sliced berries. Cover with plastic wrap and place in the freezer for at least 2 hours.

When you are ready to serve, preheat the oven to broil. Place the egg whites in an electric mixer and whip at high speed until peaks begin to form. Sprinkle in the 1 1/2 packets of Equal that remain as well as the cream of tartar and sugar. When the sugar has dissolved, add the vanilla extract and green food coloring. Beat until stiff peaks are formed.

Spread the meringue liberally on top of the ice milk, making curly peaks. Place under the broiler until the tips of the meringue are lightly browned. Drizzle 1 teaspoon of brandy on top of each dessert, light with a match, and present at once. You may have to blow the flame out to prevent it from burning the meringue. Serves 4.

Lagniappe: This is the cousin to the dish known as Baked Alaska. It is every bit as fun and much lower in calories. You can prepare the ice milk and shortcake for freezing up to 2 days in advance, but be sure to keep it tightly wrapped with plastic wrap. Just remove from the freezer and prepare as above. You can change the flavor of the ice milk, but check to see if that changes the calorie count.

Calories — 137; Carb — 33.2; Fat — 5.0; Chol — 9.0; Pro — 7.2; Fib — 0.7

FRESH STRAWBERRIES GINGER

**4 cups fresh
strawberries
2 tsp. fresh grated ginger**

**1 tbsp. fresh mint leaves,
minced
4 packets Equal sweetener**

Wash the strawberries well, remove the stems, and slice them in half. In a large bowl, toss the strawberries with the ginger and mint. Sprinkle with the Equal. Cover and chill for 6 hours. Serve chilled. Serves 4.

Lagniappe: This is sweet, colorful, and light. Berries are always an excellent dessert choice. Most people enjoy them, and the calories per serving are so low!

Calories — 50; Carb — 11.9; Fat — 0.7; Chol — 0.0; Pro — 0.9; Fib — 2.8

Index